Council Tax Nullity: How to Challenge Local Tax Demands through Honour and Law

Sovereign Action, Volume 2

Roger Davies

Published by TWON Publications, 2025.

COUNCIL TAX NULLITY: HOW TO CHALLENGE LOCAL TAX DEMANDS THROUGH HONOUR AND LAW

First edition. October 5, 2025.

ISBN: 979-8232692421

Written by Roger Davies.

Table of Contents

Dedication

This book is dedicated to every man and woman who chooses truth over fear and peace over conflict. May you find the courage to question, the patience to learn, and the honour to live freely in conscience.

All ideas shared here are for education and reflection only. They are not legal advice, but a reminder that knowledge and calmness are the true foundations of freedom.

"The law was never meant to rule the living, only to serve them. When truth is spoken with honour, no authority stands above it."

— Roger Davies

Introduction

Every household in the land receives them. Letters printed in capital letters, sealed with a council logo, declaring what must be paid and when. They arrive without agreement, without conversation, and without explanation of contract. They speak as if authority were absolute. Most people open them, sigh, and pay. They believe the demand is law. They believe silence means obedience. Yet behind those envelopes lies an illusion so complete that it has replaced truth for generations.

This book does not promise evasion or magic words. It offers understanding. When you know how the system functions, fear dissolves. When fear dissolves, honour can appear. *Council Tax Nullity* is not about rebellion. It is about recognition. It teaches how to meet official letters with awareness, how to stand in peace, and how to communicate with councils as the living being rather than the assumed corporate subject.

Council tax is often presented as a moral duty, the price of living in a civilised society. Yet morality loses meaning when choice is absent. True duty arises from consent. Every lawful relationship, whether between neighbours or nations, rests on agreement. Consent makes obligation lawful. The absence of consent makes it commercial. Councils do not explain this difference because to do so would reveal that what they call law is often administration.

To understand council tax, one must first understand the environment in which it operates. Councils are not the ancient community institutions they appear to be. They are corporations registered with company numbers, bank accounts, and directors. Their letters are not judgments of law but notices of offer within a commercial framework. The words may sound commanding, but their power depends on the same thing that sustains all commerce: acceptance. Without it, the offer remains paper.

The purpose of this book is to show how to meet such offers with honour rather than hostility. Anger feeds the system. Silence feeds it too. Only awareness removes its nourishment. By learning how to respond calmly, in writing, and with lawful questions, you shift the burden back to those who make the claim. This is not defiance. It is lawful dialogue. The man or woman who asks for proof acts in peace. The one who demands without proof acts in presumption. Law belongs to the former.

Each chapter that follows explains a different part of the process. You will see how consent is hidden within paperwork, how silence becomes agreement, and how words such as "liable," "occupier," and "resident" carry meanings far removed from common understanding. You will learn the difference between statute and law, between assumption and evidence. Most of all, you will see that peace holds more strength than protest.

Council tax, like all financial mechanisms of control, relies on the ignorance of those it targets. The system expects compliance through fear. It sends letters designed to appear final, uses language that suggests judgment, and employs courts that function more like accounting departments than seats of justice. The truth, once understood, is simple. The system cannot bind the living without consent. It can only bind the person, which is a title created on paper. The man or woman who knows this distinction begins to live differently.

To walk this path requires patience. Sovereign understanding does not grow from anger. It grows from stillness. You cannot defeat confusion with more confusion. This book therefore speaks softly. It does not shout of rights. It reminds of responsibilities. Every step you take in this process must be taken in honour. That means no aggression, no false claims, and no deceit. Peace is the strongest position you can hold.

You will learn how to write and serve lawful notices that question rather than accuse. You will see how to demand evidence of contract, proof of obligation, and confirmation of jurisdiction. You will learn why councils rarely answer such questions directly, and why their silence becomes your evidence. You will also learn the importance of keeping record, of building your private archive, and of maintaining consistency in tone.

The system you face operates by presumption. It presumes you are the name written in capital letters. It presumes you have entered contract. It presumes you accept its rules. Presumption stands only until rebutted. Your written replies provide that rebuttal. They correct the record, not through anger but through lawful communication. Once you understand that law begins with language, you will see that every letter you send is an act of education to those who receive it.

This book is not a manual for avoidance. It is a guide to honourable engagement. There is no freedom in deceit, and no dignity in aggression. The path of lawful communication brings peace because it aligns with truth. It teaches you to see behind the mask of authority and to respond as the living being, not the frightened subject. The goal is not to destroy the system but to outgrow it through awareness.

Each chapter builds upon the one before it. You will start by exploring the hidden contract behind council tax and the corporate structure of local authorities. You will then learn the difference between statute and law, followed by the role of consent, silence, and presumption. Later chapters show how to read summonses, how to serve conditional acceptances, and how to challenge jurisdiction respectfully. You will study the role of the Strawman, the meaning of liability, and the methods for rebutting assumptions of benefit. Finally, you will see examples of honourable correspondence that restored peace where conflict once ruled.

Throughout this journey, you are reminded to act in honour. The Sovereign never lies, never threatens, and never hides. Your letters should reflect truth, patience, and clarity. Even when faced with intimidation, your calmness is your authority. The council worker who reads your letter may never have met anyone who speaks this way. You are not teaching them rebellion. You are showing them humanity.

The term "nullity" in the title of this book does not mean destruction. It means recognition of what holds no lawful standing. When a thing has no lawful foundation, it is null. Council tax becomes null not because you wish it so but because the claim cannot survive examination. Every lawful system allows challenge. If challenge is silenced, the system confesses fear. Your role is not to shout at its gates but to ask questions that no one else dares to ask.

By the end of this book, you will see that true freedom from unlawful demand does not come from refusal. It comes from mastery of communication. The pen becomes your sword, but it cuts only deceit, never peace. You will learn how to hold authority accountable without hatred, how to stand without aggression, and how to speak truth so plainly that evasion becomes impossible.

Remember always that every council employee, every clerk, and every officer is also a living being. Many act from ignorance rather than malice. Treat them with respect. Your honour reflects your understanding. The more calmly you act, the more powerful your record becomes. The system cannot punish peace, and it cannot argue with truth delivered politely.

The path you are about to study is not for those who seek shortcuts. It requires reading, patience, and courage. It demands that you control emotion and master timing. Yet once you understand the principles within these pages, you will never again fear a letter from any authority. You will read it with clear eyes, reply with honour, and rest knowing that truth stands beside you.

The purpose of *Council Tax Nullity* is not to turn you against society but to restore balance between the governed and those who govern. When communication returns to equality, coercion fades. When honour replaces fear, the game ends. The power that once belonged to offices and titles returns to where it always belonged — the living man and woman.

This book invites you to walk that path, not with defiance but with dignity. Read slowly. Reflect deeply. Write only in truth. And when you serve your next notice, remember that peace is not passive. It is active awareness expressed through calm action. The Sovereign who lives by peace cannot be enslaved by paper.

Chapter 1:
The Hidden Contract Behind Council Tax

To understand council tax, you must begin with the idea of contract. Every financial relationship in the world operates on one foundation, agreement between parties. Without consent, no obligation can exist in law. This is the rule that governs trade, commerce, and fairness itself. It is the golden thread that connects honour to obligation. Yet, when it comes to council tax, that thread has been quietly cut and replaced with assumption.

Council tax is presented as law, not as agreement. The language used in letters and leaflets speaks of duty, liability, and enforcement. It never speaks of offer, acceptance, or consent. This absence is not an oversight. It is the design of a commercial system that depends on belief rather than fact. When people believe that a demand is law, they stop asking questions. The system thrives on that silence.

The first truth to recognise is that council tax operates as a contract in disguise. Councils act as corporations registered under company law. They issue invoices that appear as lawful demands but function as commercial offers. They rely on your silence as proof of acceptance. The moment you respond without awareness, you confirm the presumption that you have entered into contract.

This process begins at birth. The birth certificate creates the legal persona, a corporate identity linked to your name written in capital letters. That persona is used in all financial and governmental dealings. The council does not send letters to the living man or woman. It sends them to the persona. The system functions by treating that paper entity as the debtor, while the living being unknowingly acts as surety. Once you understand that distinction, you see the trick for what it is.

A contract requires four elements. There must be offer, acceptance, consideration, and intention to create legal relations. If any of these elements is missing, no lawful contract exists. Look at a council tax demand and ask yourself where these elements appear. The council's letter is the offer. Your silence or payment becomes acceptance. The money you send is consideration. The intention to create legal relations is presumed rather than proven. The entire process rests on presumption.

This is why notices are so important. A written notice questions those presumptions. It asks for proof of contract, proof of obligation, and evidence of consent. If the council cannot provide those proofs, its claim loses standing. You are not refusing to pay. You are asking to see the foundation of the demand. This is not rebellion. It is lawful procedure.

When you write to the council, you act as an equal, not as a subject. You are communicating with another corporation that must obey the same rules of commerce as any business. The council, though presented as a public authority, is still a legal person that can enter into contracts, hold accounts, and be challenged through correspondence. The relationship only feels unequal because you were never told that you could question it.

Examine a typical council tax bill. You will notice that it contains no signature from any officer taking personal responsibility. It is printed by computer and bears only the name of the council. In law, an unsigned document carries no verified authority. A man or woman must stand behind every claim. When no signature appears, the claim exists only as assumption. That assumption is what most people mistake for law.

To expose this hidden contract, you must learn to read with discernment. Words such as "liable," "must," and "enforcement" are commercial triggers. They are designed to create urgency and fear. Yet none of them changes the basic rule of law: no contract, no obligation. A true lawful demand must show the basis of agreement. It must include the name and authority of the claimant, the terms of contract, and the consent of both parties. Council tax demands contain none of these things.

The deception is maintained through repetition. Every year, the letters arrive. The format never changes. The tone remains firm. Over time, familiarity becomes belief. People stop questioning because they assume the process has been tested and proven. Yet belief is not evidence. A thousand repetitions of error do not turn error into truth. The system survives because it hides in routine.

This understanding does not mean hostility toward councils. Many employees working within these organisations believe they are acting lawfully. They follow training, not truth. Your task is not to attack them but to remind them of their obligations. When you ask for proof of contract, you are not being difficult. You are restoring balance to a relationship that has drifted into presumption.

The hidden contract also operates through registration. When you move into a property and register for utilities, your information is shared across databases. The council assumes that occupation equals liability. It presumes that because you use services, you have agreed to payment. Yet nowhere in law does use of a public service automatically create a private contract. The obligation arises only when consent is proven. Silence is not consent. Presence is not consent. Only clear agreement is.

The lawful way to challenge this presumption is through written correspondence conducted in peace. You begin by acknowledging receipt of the council's letter and expressing willingness to settle any lawful obligation. Then you ask for proof of claim. You require evidence of contract, evidence of consent, and identification of the living man or woman making the claim. If no reply comes, the silence confirms absence of proof. That absence reveals the nullity of the demand.

Every council operates within commercial frameworks. They have credit ratings, debt collectors, and revenue departments. These are not characteristics of government in the traditional sense. They are features of business. The only difference between a council and a corporation is branding. Both rely on the same law of contract. Both require consent. Once you see this, the illusion of authority begins to fade.

The language of law often conceals rather than reveals. Words are chosen to obscure meaning. For example, the term "summons" in council tax proceedings does not refer to a criminal summons under common law. It refers to a commercial invitation to attend a hearing. The court used in such cases is usually an administrative office, not a court of record. This distinction is critical. The entire process is commercial, yet it is presented as judicial.

Your strength lies in clarity. When you act with understanding, confusion cannot control you. Each letter you write, each question you ask, reclaims ground from presumption. You do not need to shout about rights or threaten action. You need only to demand proof. The more calmly you do so, the more the system struggles to respond. Bureaucracy cannot handle individuality. It thrives only on predictable obedience.

Understanding the hidden contract also reveals the moral question. True community requires contribution, but contribution must be voluntary. When councils demand payment under threat, they destroy the very morality they claim to uphold. Law without consent is tyranny, even when it hides behind good intentions. The Sovereign does not reject contribution. He or she insists that it be based on fairness and transparency.

You may ask why no one challenges this system publicly. The answer is simple. Fear. Those who speak out are labelled troublemakers. Those who comply are rewarded with convenience. Yet history shows that truth always begins as minority voice. Change does not come from noise but from persistence. Every notice you write plants a seed of awareness. Each act of peace weakens the hold of deception.

Your goal is not to avoid responsibility but to define it. You decide what is fair, lawful, and aligned with conscience. You cannot outsource that duty to councils or governments. Responsibility is the foundation of sovereignty. Without it, freedom becomes chaos. By questioning unlawful demands, you are not escaping duty. You are fulfilling it.

The chapters that follow will explore how to apply these principles in practical form. You will learn how councils function as corporations, how statute differs from law, and how consent operates through silence. You will see how to interpret every letter as a commercial offer and how to reply with conditional acceptance. You will learn how to remain in honour even under pressure.

Once you grasp the truth of the hidden contract, fear will never again guide your choices. You will read every demand with calm eyes, knowing that no piece of paper can claim ownership of a living being. Authority that depends on ignorance is not law. It is performance. The moment you stop believing in it, the play ends.

Once you recognise that council tax is a commercial arrangement disguised as obligation, your perception of authority begins to shift. The letters no longer seem powerful. They are revealed as proposals written in formal tone. The threat behind them loses weight because it relies entirely on consent. You begin to see that power in modern governance does not come from law but from belief.

The hidden contract continues through every stage of the collection process. The council sends reminders, final notices, and summonses, each worded to suggest escalation. The design is psychological rather than lawful. The language aims to create fear of loss. Fear compels compliance faster than any statute. The entire sequence depends on one thing, your reaction. The moment you respond in panic, you confirm their presumption of authority. The moment you respond in peace, you expose its absence.

Behind each demand is a chain of assumptions. The first is that you are the person named. The second is that you have accepted benefit. The third is that you are subject to the statute that created the charge. All three are beliefs, not evidence. None of them can stand when challenged in honour. The living man or woman is not the corporate name. Use of water, light, or waste services does not create private contract. Statutes apply only by consent. These truths remain hidden because few ever question them.

Councils operate within the law of agency. Their powers derive from statute, not from divine or natural authority. That means their actions must follow procedure precisely. A single error in process renders a demand void. Yet most recipients never read past the first line. They see the words "final notice" and surrender. The Sovereign reads every word, searches every definition, and asks the questions that silence fear.

One of the most effective ways to reveal the hidden contract is to ask for identification of the claimant. The council acts through officers and departments, but who, in law, is making the claim? A living being must take responsibility for any lawful statement. When you ask this question, you challenge the mask of office. Bureaucracy has no answer because no individual wants to bear liability. The claim therefore remains unverified. Without verification, it cannot stand.

Another question concerns evidence of contract. You may ask, "Please provide a copy of the agreement bearing the signatures of both parties that proves my obligation." The council cannot produce such a document because no such contract exists. Their silence on this matter reveals the nullity of their position. It is not defiance to ask for proof. It is honourable enquiry. Every legitimate system should welcome it.

Keep all correspondence respectful and factual. Insults, threats, or emotional language weaken your position. The strength of your letter lies in its calm tone and clarity. State your willingness to settle any lawful obligation, then request proof that one exists. This approach removes aggression while maintaining firmness. It transforms confrontation into lawful process.

The hidden contract also appears in the court system used for council tax. These hearings often take place in rooms that resemble courts but are administrative offices. The clerk reads from a script, and decisions are made in bulk. There is no judge in the traditional sense, no record of evidence, and no recognition of the living man or woman. The process is mechanical, designed for speed rather than justice. It functions only because participants believe it is binding.

In truth, no living man or woman is compelled to participate in a commercial proceeding without consent. Attendance is voluntary, though the language of the summons implies compulsion. The word "summons" itself has been redefined. In ancient law, a summons required personal notice from a court of record. In administrative practice, it means invitation. You are invited to confirm or challenge an account. Understanding that distinction removes fear.

If you choose to attend such a hearing, you do so as observer, not defendant. You may state that you are present to settle any lawful obligation upon proof of claim. You do not argue or resist. You stand in honour. The atmosphere in such rooms often changes when a calm, well-informed individual speaks with confidence. Officials are unaccustomed to peaceful challenge. Their routine depends on submission. When you act in peace, the machinery slows.

It is important to remember that honour is not weakness. Honour means strength under control. You do not allow frustration to dictate behaviour. The system expects anger and labels it as rebellion. It has no response to calm truth. The hidden contract loses force the moment you refuse to play its emotional game.

Many who study this path discover that councils often withdraw quietly once challenged in writing. They may stop replying, pass the matter to third-party collectors, or issue generic responses that avoid questions. This silence is not defeat for you. It is confirmation of absence of proof. Record it. Every unanswered letter becomes evidence that the claim lacks lawful foundation. The purpose of your correspondence is not to win argument but to create record of truth.

Understanding this hidden structure also brings moral responsibility. Knowledge should never be used to exploit or deceive. The goal is balance, not manipulation. You do not refuse genuine obligations such as agreements you knowingly entered. You challenge only what is imposed without consent. Lawful living requires discernment. Use what you learn to restore fairness, not to escape it.

The concept of "nullity" is not about destruction but correction. When a claim lacks proof, it collapses under its own weight. You need not fight it. You simply remove belief from it. This is why the written record is so important. Your letters document the process of correction. They show that you acted with honour, asked fair questions, and offered peaceful remedy.

The hidden contract thrives on three weaknesses: fear, ignorance, and apathy. Fear silences inquiry. Ignorance blinds understanding. Apathy sustains both. Once you replace these with knowledge, patience, and courage, the illusion breaks. Councils depend on collective compliance. Individual awareness disrupts that dependence. You do not need to convince anyone else. You need only to act in peace yourself.

You may find resistance from friends or family who cannot see what you now see. They will repeat what they have been taught, that council tax is law, that refusal brings punishment. Be patient with them. Remember that truth cannot be forced. Those who are ready will understand in their own time. Your calm example teaches more than argument ever could.

In time, you will notice subtle changes in how you perceive all official correspondence. Letters that once caused anxiety will appear as opportunities to practise honour. You will read every word slowly, translate the commercial language into plain truth, and decide your response deliberately. This habit extends beyond council tax. It transforms how you live. You begin to treat every interaction, written or spoken, as a potential contract. You choose which to accept. You choose which to decline.

The deeper purpose of exposing the hidden contract is self-knowledge. Each time you challenge a presumption, you reaffirm that authority begins within. External systems mirror internal understanding. The more you trust conscience, the less you depend on external permission. This is the true meaning of sovereignty. It is not rebellion against others. It is mastery of self.

By the end of this book, you will have learned to recognise every letter, statement, and notice as a form of communication seeking your agreement. Some deserve acceptance. Others deserve silence. The power lies in choice. Councils cannot compel consent. They can only request it in coded form. Once you see through that code, you are no longer bound by it.

The hidden contract behind council tax reveals a larger truth about modern society. Much of what appears as governance is commerce in disguise. The same pattern repeats across all institutions, from banks to courts to governments. Understanding one example opens the door to all others. Awareness in one area spreads to every part of life.

This first chapter has shown that council tax rests on assumption, not law. It functions only because the living forget their own authority. The chapters ahead will show how to uncover that truth in action. You will learn to identify corporate behaviour in councils, to read statutes as contracts, and to use written notice as the tool of peace. Knowledge is your safeguard. Peace is your strength.

Chapter 2:
How Local Authorities Operate as Corporations

When most people hear the word "council," they picture community service, public good, and neighbourly governance. They imagine men and women working for local benefit under the guidance of law. Yet when you examine how local authorities truly function, a different picture appears. Behind the language of service stands the machinery of commerce. Councils are not guardians of the people. They are corporate entities that operate according to the same financial principles as private business.

A corporation is a legal person created by registration. It is born on paper. It possesses a name, an address, and a registration number. It can own property, make contracts, borrow money, and be sued. Yet it is not alive. It acts through agents, officers, and employees. Local authorities fit this description precisely. They are registered bodies with trading status, accounts, and financial obligations. Their first duty is not to truth but to solvency. The living man or woman who understands this sees that the relationship between council and resident is not moral but commercial.

Every council in the United Kingdom has a corporate registration. These details can be found through Companies House or other public databases. The council's name will often include words such as "borough," "district," or "authority," but its status remains that of a registered corporation. It has directors, departments, and trading activities. It may issue bonds, hold investments, and engage in joint ventures. When it sends a bill or demand, it does so as a commercial entity seeking payment.

Understanding this structure changes everything. The letters you receive are not communications from government in the ancient sense. They are notices from a company operating under statutory licence. The employees who sign those letters act as agents of that company. Their authority exists only within that role. Outside of it, they are ordinary men and women. The council's power ends where your consent begins.

A corporation cannot act without consent. It cannot compel performance from a living being without agreement. What it can do is offer terms, present documents that appear mandatory, and rely on the public's assumption of obligation. This method is not unique to councils. It is the same model used by banks, insurance firms, and all corporate institutions. The difference is that councils hide behind the appearance of government. The badge and the logo create an illusion of authority that most never question.

To reveal the commercial nature of councils, examine their financial reports. Every year they publish statements of accounts, budgets, and investment strategies. These documents show income from council tax, business rates, and government grants. They also show expenditures on wages, loans, and contracts. The language is identical to that of any company. Profit may not be stated directly, but surplus and deficit are tracked carefully. This is the vocabulary of commerce, not of law.

When a corporation issues a demand for payment, it acts as creditor. Yet for a debt to exist, there must be a contract. The council assumes that registration of a property or occupancy creates that contract. It does not. Registration merely records information. It does not form agreement. Without explicit consent, the council's claim remains an offer, not an obligation. This is why your written response matters. By asking for evidence of contract, you shift the relationship from assumption to accountability.

The corporate model also explains the aggressive tone of council communication. Employees are trained in revenue collection, not law. Their purpose is to meet financial targets. Each department has performance goals measured in income recovered, cases closed, and arrears reduced. The moral language used in public announcements hides a business plan. This is not governance by principle. It is administration by profit.

Even the use of courts reflects corporate practice. When councils take cases to the magistrates' court, they pay a fee to secure liability orders in bulk. These orders are then used as instruments of debt recovery. The court functions as extension of the revenue department, processing paperwork rather than judging law. The system resembles an assembly line. Once again, the process is commercial, not judicial.

Councils maintain public confidence through branding. Logos, uniforms, and formal titles create the impression of legitimacy. Yet these symbols have no inherent authority. They derive their power from recognition. When people believe in the symbol, they obey it. When they question it, the illusion fades. This is why the Sovereign always remains respectful. The goal is not to destroy the symbol but to understand it. When you see it clearly, you are no longer controlled by it.

Many people working within councils do not realise they serve a corporation. They believe they are part of public service. This belief keeps the system stable. It allows ordinary men and women to act as administrators of contracts they do not understand. When you communicate with them in peace and honour, some begin to question the structure themselves. Your calmness becomes a mirror that reveals truth.

The structure of a local authority mirrors that of any large company. At the top is the chief executive, who functions like a managing director. Below them are directors of departments such as finance, housing, and environment. Each department has managers, officers, and clerks. Every role is defined by procedure. Each employee follows written policy rather than personal conscience. This hierarchy ensures consistency but removes individual responsibility. No one at any level claims liability for error because responsibility is diffused across the structure.

The corporate model also means that councils can be challenged through standard commercial procedures. You can request information under freedom of information laws, question the source of their authority, and ask for details of their registration. You can communicate with the chief executive directly, as the head of the corporation. When you write, address them as the accountable officer. These actions remind the organisation that it operates under the same law of commerce as any other company.

Understanding this structure helps you remain calm during correspondence. You realise that the person sending the letter is following instruction, not conscience. There is no need for anger. You address the institution as a corporate body and the employee as a fellow living being. This distinction keeps you in honour. It also protects you from emotional manipulation.

You will notice that councils frequently use third-party collection agencies. These agencies are separate companies acting as contractors. Their letters use threatening language to provoke payment. Yet every such demand relies on the original contract. If the council cannot prove obligation, neither can its agent. Each collector becomes a secondary claimant operating without foundation. The correct response is always the same, calm request for proof of lawful contract.

The registration of councils as corporations also explains why they engage in business activities unrelated to local governance. Many invest in property, technology, or private ventures. Some borrow millions to fund development schemes. These actions show where their true priorities lie. A lawful government serves life. A corporation serves profit. This is not moral judgment but structural fact.

When you understand that councils operate as corporations, fear of their letters disappears. You no longer see them as moral authorities but as businesses seeking revenue. You recognise that your power lies in awareness. A business cannot compel its customers without agreement. A government should not compel its citizens without law. When the two merge, deception begins.

Knowledge of this structure also deepens compassion. You realise that the employees who send demands or threats often do so out of ignorance. They believe they are enforcing law. They have never been shown the difference between law and policy. When you respond with patience and kindness, you remind them that conscience still matters. Many are quietly relieved to encounter someone who speaks with reason rather than hostility.

The more you study the commercial structure of councils, the clearer the pattern becomes. Every policy, payment, and procedure leads back to finance. Meetings revolve around budgets, not justice. The highest concern is always the balance sheet. The word "public service" is used to describe financial management. The reality is that the council acts as financial intermediary between government grants and private contractors. It is a broker of services, not a provider of care.

This understanding is not meant to create cynicism but clarity. You cannot interact lawfully with any system you do not understand. Once you recognise the corporate model, you know how to communicate within it. You learn to use the language of commerce to restore fairness. You send written notices, make lawful requests, and hold officers accountable through the same principles they use against others.

The next chapter will explain how statute differs from law and why councils rely on confusion between the two. You will see that what most people call law is often policy written in persuasive language. Once you understand this difference, you will be able to distinguish between moral duty and commercial obligation. That distinction is the key to peace and the foundation of lawful living.

Understanding councils as corporations transforms how you interpret every action they take. Once you remove the illusion of moral authority, their behaviour begins to make sense. You see that their decisions are driven by financial strategy, not public duty. When a council cuts services or increases charges, it does so for the same reason any company does, to manage profit and loss. The appearance of democracy hides the mathematics of commerce.

Each department within a local authority functions like a business division. Housing deals in assets, waste management in contracts, and finance in investment. Every service becomes a cost centre, measured by revenue and expenditure. Employees are trained to achieve efficiency targets, not to protect rights. The idea of serving the people has been replaced by the goal of sustaining the corporation.

This structure explains the language used in official correspondence. Terms such as "customer," "client," and "service user" have replaced "resident" or "citizen." The relationship is no longer one of trust between community and caretaker but one of transaction between supplier and consumer. Council tax is framed as payment for service, yet no individual agreement exists. The illusion of contract is maintained by repetition, not consent.

Once you see this clearly, fear gives way to awareness. The council is not a moral authority. It is a commercial body making an offer of service. You are not a subject. You are a potential customer. The difference is profound. A subject obeys. A customer chooses. By accepting or declining that offer in peace, you reclaim control of your affairs.

The corporate structure also reveals why councils avoid taking personal responsibility. Within commerce, liability is always limited. That principle protects directors and employees from the consequences of their actions. When you ask an officer to take personal accountability for a claim, they often refuse or remain silent. Their silence is not arrogance. It is fear of liability. No one wishes to stand personally responsible for a demand that cannot be proven.

When you communicate with councils, always address your letters to a named individual. Doing so transfers responsibility from the organisation to the living being acting as its agent. This small act restores balance. You are no longer speaking to a faceless institution. You are addressing a man or woman who must answer in honour. This change in tone has great effect. Bureaucracy cannot hide easily behind procedure when faced with personal accountability.

Each local authority also maintains financial links with central government and private contractors. Funding arrives through grants, subsidies, and loans. Expenditure flows to companies that provide goods and services. The council acts as intermediary. Money moves through it but rarely remains within it. This constant flow keeps the corporation dependent on income. Without steady collection from council tax, its financial model collapses. This dependency explains its aggressive pursuit of payment. It is not enforcing law. It is maintaining cash flow.

When you respond to council letters, remember this economic pressure. You are not confronting morality. You are questioning a business model. The employee who writes to you has been trained to protect revenue. They see each payment as target achieved and each challenge as risk to balance. Understanding this context allows you to remain calm. You no longer take their tone personally. You see it as the product of a system built on fear of financial loss.

A corporation survives through contract. Every transaction must rest on agreement, even if that agreement is assumed. Councils rely on silence to create the appearance of consent. Each year they send notices expecting no reply. Those who question are rare. That rarity gives you strength. A single act of lawful enquiry stands out within a structure built on automatic compliance. When you ask questions, you introduce truth into a world of routine.

Corporate law recognises the importance of disclosure. A company must always act transparently when entering a contract. If a council cannot provide clear evidence of the terms and parties involved, no lawful contract exists. When you ask for that evidence, you are not being difficult. You are inviting transparency. Those who act in truth will welcome such enquiry. Those who act in deceit will avoid it. Their response, or lack of it, reveals which they are.

The commercial identity of councils is also evident in their use of debt collection agencies. These agencies purchase or manage alleged debts for profit. They are not agents of justice but traders in paper claims. Each relies on fear to secure payment. Yet they possess no greater authority than the council itself. Their letters and phone calls are attempts to negotiate contract through intimidation. A calm request for proof of obligation often ends their pursuit. They cannot provide what does not exist.

The corporate mindset also explains why councils treat objections as administrative inconvenience rather than lawful challenge. To them, every question delays process. Their focus is efficiency, not truth. They measure success by how many cases are closed, not by whether justice was served. Understanding this helps you frame your communication clearly. You must write in a way that cannot be filed away easily. Each notice must demand a specific answer that exposes responsibility.

The illusion of authority is maintained through presentation. Uniforms, emblems, and titles create the sense of power. Yet these symbols carry meaning only through belief. When you respond in writing, you strip the exchange of those symbols. The conversation returns to language. In that realm, equality is restored. The council officer and the Sovereign correspondent stand as two living beings communicating through words. The titles lose meaning. Truth remains.

It is important to keep record of all your correspondence. Every letter you send or receive becomes part of your private archive. In commercial law, the record is the foundation of evidence. Councils rely on digital systems that record only their perspective. Your private archive balances that record with your version of truth. Over time, it becomes your protection. It shows that you acted in honour, asked for evidence, and offered remedy.

Some people become disillusioned when they realise how corporate the system has become. They feel betrayed by institutions they once trusted. Yet awareness should not lead to bitterness. The system reflects the collective state of society. As long as people value convenience over responsibility, commerce will dominate governance. Change begins not with anger but with example. Each individual who lives lawfully and communicates honourably contributes to a gradual return to fairness.

This chapter's purpose is not to condemn councils but to reveal their nature. Once you see them as corporations, your approach changes. You no longer plead or resist. You communicate as equal. You ask questions, demand clarity, and remain polite. You do not seek victory but truth. The corporate structure cannot handle sustained honesty because it thrives on procedure, not conscience. Your words become tests of integrity.

When you write to a council, remember that your letter is not only correspondence but education. Each officer who reads it learns something about honour, even if they do not reply. You plant seeds of awareness within a system that has forgotten what service truly means. Whether they grow immediately or slowly does not matter. Truth always finds its way into the light.

The corporate identity of councils also offers a path for remedy. A corporation can be held accountable for dishonour in commerce. Written notice, served properly, creates lawful record. If the corporation continues to act without evidence, it commits fraud by silence. The man or woman who keeps full record of correspondence possesses proof of that dishonour. The purpose of this knowledge is not revenge but protection. Awareness prevents exploitation.

The next chapter will explore how statute differs from law. You will learn that statute governs corporations and persons, while law governs the living. Understanding that difference will show why councils depend on your identification with the legal persona rather than the living being. When you know who you are, you cannot be compelled by paper.

Chapter 3:
Statute versus Law

The greatest confusion in modern society arises from the failure to distinguish statute from law. The two are spoken of as if they were the same, yet they differ in nature, origin, and effect. Law is eternal. Statute is temporal. Law expresses the principles that protect life, peace, and fairness. Statute expresses the policies that serve administration. One arises from conscience. The other arises from government. Understanding this distinction is the key to freedom from presumption.

A statute is a rule made by men and women acting as legislators. It has authority only over those who consent to be bound by it. Law, in contrast, exists without signature or vote. It requires no parliament to declare it and no judge to confirm it. Law simply is. When a man or woman harms another, the wrong exists whether or not it has been written down. When no harm occurs, no lawful claim can stand. This principle forms the basis of all true justice.

Councils operate entirely within the realm of statute. Their authority begins and ends with acts of parliament. Without those statutes, they have no existence. The buildings, departments, and officers rely on written policy, not conscience. That is why their correspondence reads as instruction rather than invitation. Statute speaks in commands because it assumes obedience. Law speaks in truth because it assumes conscience.

When you receive a council tax demand, it cites the Local Government Finance Act and other statutory instruments. These are not laws in the natural sense. They are policies created by government for the management of persons. They operate in the commercial domain, not the lawful one. The living man or woman is governed by conscience, not by policy. The legal person, which is the corporate name, is governed by statute. Confusion between the two creates the illusion of universal authority.

To see the difference, consider how enforcement operates. A statute requires enforcement officers, fines, and penalties to ensure obedience. Law requires none of these. The natural consequences of harm or deceit are sufficient. When someone steals, harm is evident, and justice arises naturally. When someone breaks a statute without causing harm, the offence exists only in writing. It is administrative, not moral.

This distinction explains why councils rely heavily on paperwork. They must create the appearance of lawful process through forms, notices, and summonses. Yet without consent, these remain proposals. A statute applies only when the individual accepts the role of person created by it. The man or woman who stands as living being does not enter that role unless they choose to. This is the essence of lawful independence.

Law belongs to the living. It is universal, unchanging, and self-evident. It can be expressed in a few simple maxims. Do no harm. Cause no loss. Commit no fraud. Keep the peace. These are the boundaries that protect freedom while preserving order. They require no legislation to exist. The child who lies knows instinctively that truth has value. The adult who breaks promise feels the weight of conscience. This is law.

Statute, however, must be written and maintained. It changes with every government, expands with every crisis, and multiplies beyond understanding. Its complexity creates dependence. Those who cannot interpret it rely on experts to explain it. This dependence breeds control. Law liberates through simplicity. Statute enslaves through confusion. The one who understands the difference sees through the fog of authority.

When councils act, they do so as agents of statute. They invoke sections, paragraphs, and subsections to justify demands. Yet when asked for evidence of lawful contract, they fall silent. The reason is simple. Law cannot be proven through statute. The two operate in separate domains. Statute governs corporate relationships. Law governs living beings. The moment you stand as living man or woman, the council's authority diminishes to mere offer.

Understanding this does not mean rejecting all statutes. Some express lawful principles and serve genuine public good. The difference lies in consent. When you agree voluntarily, the statute becomes useful tool. When you are coerced, it becomes instrument of control. The Sovereign chooses consciously when to accept and when to decline. Choice defines freedom.

You can test the difference by asking a simple question. Does compliance prevent harm, or does it serve administration? If the answer is prevention of harm, the rule aligns with law. If it serves only procedure, it belongs to statute. Council tax belongs to the latter. Its purpose is to fund administration, not to prevent harm. It is therefore commercial in nature.

When writing to councils, refer always to the distinction between lawful obligation and statutory requirement. You might write, "I am willing to settle any lawful claim upon proof of obligation." This statement respects law while questioning statute. It keeps you in honour while exposing presumption. Councils can operate only when people blur this line. By keeping it clear, you protect yourself without conflict.

The confusion between statute and law is maintained through education. Schools teach obedience to rules but rarely teach the nature of law. People grow up believing that legality equals morality. They assume that written code defines right and wrong. This conditioning makes control simple. A society that equates compliance with virtue will enforce its own chains. The Sovereign breaks that habit by returning to conscience.

In conversation, you may meet those who insist that statute is law because parliament says so. They forget that parliament itself derives authority from the consent of the governed. Without that consent, its words are mere ink. Power exists only through recognition. The man or woman who withdraws recognition peacefully reclaims that power. No conflict is needed. Silence and clarity achieve more than protest.

Statute serves a purpose in managing large populations. It provides structure where conscience has grown weak. Yet it should never replace natural law. When it does, justice becomes procedure, and truth becomes policy. The restoration of balance begins when individuals act from honour rather than fear. Councils will continue to issue demands as long as people obey automatically. The moment enough individuals respond with reason, the system must evolve.

Some may argue that without statute there would be chaos. The opposite is true. Statute creates dependence on enforcement. Law creates self-regulation. A society guided by conscience requires fewer rules. The complexity of modern governance reveals the absence of honour, not its presence. The Sovereign does not reject rules but transcends them through responsibility.

To apply this understanding in daily life, practise awareness in small matters. Notice when you act from conscience and when you act from fear of rule. When you choose the former, you live under law. When you choose the latter, you submit to statute. Gradually, conscience will guide more of your actions. Freedom grows from consistent choice, not grand declaration.

This chapter is not an attack on legislation but an invitation to think. The written word gains power only when accepted without question. By asking, "Does this rule serve life or control?" you restore your place within the natural order. You become participant rather than subject.

Statute and law will always coexist. The challenge is to know which governs which. Law must remain the master, statute the servant. When the servant rules the master, tyranny begins. Councils, acting as servants of statute, forget that they serve living communities. The Sovereign reminds them, not through rebellion but through example. Each honourable letter you write teaches that lesson silently.

The next section will explore how consent and silence shape these relationships. You will learn how authority uses silence as proof of agreement and how to reclaim that silence as power through clear communication. Once you master that principle, you will see that control over your life depends not on what others demand but on what you accept.

To live under law is to live consciously. To live under statute is to live by habit. The difference lies not in paper but in awareness. When you know the source of authority, you can choose your relationship with it. The man or woman who understands this no longer fears letters or officials. They see beyond appearance to structure. They recognise that statute depends entirely on their participation.

Statute rules only through consent. It requires the people to identify as persons, to answer to names written in capital letters, and to respond as entities created by government. Without that identification, statute loses power. Law, by contrast, applies to all living beings equally. It is the same for king and servant, judge and farmer. It makes no distinction between title and truth. This equality is what gives law its permanence.

Councils rely on the public's confusion between the two. They send letters quoting statutes as if they were moral law. They know most people will never question the difference. The result is a population that obeys procedure as if it were justice. When the Sovereign receives such a letter, they read carefully. They separate lawful principle from statutory policy. They reply with questions that expose assumption.

Understanding this difference also clarifies the meaning of punishment. Under law, punishment exists to restore balance. It seeks to correct harm. Under statute, punishment exists to enforce obedience. It serves the system rather than the individual. When a council threatens fines or enforcement, it acts not to restore harmony but to preserve income. Recognising this removes moral guilt from your challenge. You are not refusing duty. You are questioning procedure.

A lawful society requires both conscience and structure. Statute can assist when used properly. It can provide order for large groups who share common needs. But when statute replaces conscience entirely, it becomes a tool of control. Councils often act as if statute grants them divine right. Yet statute is nothing more than written instruction for corporate function. It has meaning only when living beings choose to follow it.

The reason statute feels powerful is that it operates through the fear of consequence. People obey to avoid penalty. True law operates through conscience. People act rightly because it feels correct. The first requires threat. The second requires understanding. The goal of the Sovereign is to move from fear to understanding, from compulsion to choice.

One of the most effective ways to reveal this distinction in practice is through conditional acceptance. When a council issues a statutory demand, you may write, "I am willing to settle any lawful claim upon proof of obligation." This statement honours law while questioning statute. It places responsibility back on the claimant to prove the rule applies. Those acting in truth will respond with evidence. Those acting in assumption will avoid the question. Their silence becomes record of dishonour.

You will find that officials often respond with form letters quoting legislation. These letters never address your questions directly. They repeat statutory references as if repetition equals proof. This is not deceit but habit. The employees have been trained to follow script, not logic. They believe that citation of statute ends discussion. When you reply calmly, asking again for lawful evidence, you introduce reason into routine. The system struggles to respond to reason because it has forgotten how.

Law lives through conscience. Statute survives through compliance. The two are not enemies, but they must remain distinct. When you live by conscience, statute becomes tool rather than master. You use it where it serves fairness and ignore it where it violates honour. This selective awareness turns obedience into discipline. You no longer act from fear of rule but from love of order.

In modern governance, most officials act as enforcers of policy, not as guardians of law. Their role is administrative, not moral. They ensure that revenue flows and records remain consistent. This is not evil. It is mechanical. When you understand this, you stop personalising authority. You see the system as machine rather than monster. Machines respond to input. Your letters are that input. Each one changes the record.

The danger of confusing statute with law lies in the erosion of personal responsibility. When people believe that written rules absolve them of conscience, they become instruments of harm. History offers countless examples of atrocities committed by those who claimed to be "following orders." Law without conscience becomes tyranny in uniform. The Sovereign rejects that excuse. You remain responsible for your actions even when acting under policy.

This is why written record matters. It proves that you acted from conscience, not defiance. When you question a demand, you do so not to evade but to understand. Your notices show that you offered remedy and sought truth. This evidence protects you from accusation and teaches those who read it that law still lives through honour.

Statute changes constantly because it serves commerce, which never rests. Law remains still because it serves life, which endures. The more you align with law, the calmer you become. You stop reacting to every new rule or policy. You measure each by its effect on peace. If it increases harmony, you accept it. If it creates confusion or fear, you question it. This simple test will guide you more surely than any book of regulations.

Living under law also restores equality in communication. When you write to an official, you write as one living being to another. Titles disappear. Authority becomes mutual respect. The conversation shifts from command to understanding. This change in tone often surprises those who receive your letters. It disarms hostility. People are used to confrontation or submission, not calm equality.

The understanding of statute and law also shapes how you view courts. True courts of record operate under law. Administrative courts operate under statute. The difference lies in the presence of a jury, the oath of the judge, and the record of evidence. Council tax hearings belong to the administrative category. They are commercial proceedings, not courts of record. Recognising this allows you to act appropriately. You engage only through written correspondence, never through emotional argument.

Statute and law coexist because both are reflections of human nature. Law reflects conscience. Statute reflects control. Society needs both until understanding matures. The Sovereign does not seek to destroy statute but to remind it of its place. It is servant, not master. When you live by that truth, you no longer need rebellion. Peace becomes your form of protest.

You may share this knowledge with others, but do so with patience. Many will resist. The belief that statute equals law is deeply rooted. People find comfort in certainty, even when false. Allow them to awaken in their own time. Your calmness will do more than your words. The living example of peace carries more authority than any explanation.

To live in accordance with law is to live in harmony with life itself. You become less concerned with victory and more concerned with balance. You act honourably because it preserves peace. This is the essence of lawful living. It requires no membership, no doctrine, and no external validation. It requires only self-awareness.

The next chapter will explore how consent and silence create the foundation of every presumed obligation. You will see how councils turn silence into agreement and how to reclaim that silence as your own. Once you understand the power of consent, you will never again be trapped by assumption.

Chapter 4:
The Role of Consent and Silence

Consent is the foundation of all lawful relationship. Without it, every claim becomes presumption and every contract becomes illusion. Yet in the modern system, consent has been hidden beneath routine. People obey rules without understanding how obedience is created. They reply to letters without recognising that reply as acceptance. They remain silent without knowing that silence itself has meaning. The system depends on that ignorance.

To live lawfully, you must understand consent in all its forms. It can be given through words, through action, or through silence. In commerce, silence is often taken as agreement. If an offer is made and not challenged within reasonable time, the offer stands accepted. This principle, though fair in trade, becomes weapon when applied to governance. Councils and institutions use it to bind those who never agreed. They send letters filled with assumptions, wait for silence, and record that silence as consent.

Every council tax demand operates on this principle. The letter arrives declaring what you owe. You do nothing. The council interprets that nothing as acceptance. A contract is presumed, and enforcement begins. In truth, no contract exists because no conscious consent was given. Yet without challenge, presumption hardens into record. Silence becomes the author of slavery.

To reclaim authority, you must replace silence with communication. The written notice is your voice. It corrects the record and removes presumption. When you respond in peace, you interrupt the automatic process that turns assumption into agreement. You restore the need for proof. The council can no longer act as if consent were given because the record now shows otherwise.

Consent must always be conscious. For agreement to be lawful, both parties must understand the terms, the consequences, and the identities involved. Councils never disclose these fully. They send unsigned letters, refer to statutes rather than contracts, and avoid naming any living claimant. Without full disclosure, consent cannot exist. This makes every unchallenged demand a deception by omission.

Silence has power because it creates space for presumption. In a busy world, most people treat letters from authorities as background noise. They pay without thought or ignore through fear. The system counts on both reactions. Payment confirms agreement. Silence confirms consent. Only communication breaks the spell. That is why the Sovereign always responds, not with anger but with questions. Questions remove assumption. Assumption cannot survive enquiry.

Understanding the role of consent also changes how you read your own actions. You begin to see where you have given agreement unknowingly. Signing forms, registering property, or updating details all carry implications. Each creates a link between the living being and the legal persona. Awareness does not mean avoiding all forms of registration. It means knowing what each signature represents. When you sign, do so consciously. When you disagree, remain silent only when silence cannot be twisted into acceptance.

The practice of lawful living therefore requires balance. There are times when silence is powerful. When no offer or presumption exists, silence preserves peace. When an offer carries assumption, silence becomes dangerous. You must decide which applies. The key is awareness. Read every communication carefully. Ask yourself whether it presumes consent. If it does, correct it through notice. If it does not, rest in silence.

In commerce, time limits are used to create pressure. Offers often include statements such as "failure to respond within seven days will be taken as agreement." Councils use similar wording in demands. These time frames have no lawful force over the living unless accepted. They are invitations to contract. You may acknowledge receipt without accepting terms. A simple response stating that you require proof of obligation removes presumption of consent while maintaining honour.

Many people fear responding to councils because they believe response gives jurisdiction. The opposite is true when written correctly. A lawful reply does not create jurisdiction. It clarifies boundaries. Jurisdiction arises from contract. When you ask for proof of contract, you are confirming that none exists until evidence appears. Silence leaves the door open. Communication closes it gently.

Consent is also withdrawn through notice. If you discover that an organisation has acted upon your assumed agreement, you may issue a notice of withdrawal of consent. This document states that you no longer permit use of your details or authority for the purpose claimed. Once served, it becomes part of the record. Future action without consent becomes dishonour. This method is not confrontation but correction. It restores equilibrium.

Silence is often mistaken for peace. In truth, silence without awareness is passivity. Peace is active. It is the deliberate choice not to fight while standing firmly in truth. When you reply to a council with honour, you are not creating conflict. You are expressing peace in motion. That is lawful strength. It confuses those trained to expect either submission or aggression.

Officials often rely on templates that assume lack of challenge. When your letter arrives, their process falters. They may send a general reply avoiding your questions. Record that reply. It proves that they received your notice yet failed to answer substance. In law, such avoidance confirms dishonour. The silence of substance is as revealing as the silence of words. Both show lack of evidence.

You will notice that the idea of consent governs every aspect of society. From taxation to medicine, from employment to technology, systems seek permission through assumption. Each form, each checkbox, each click carries contractual meaning. The living being who acts consciously transforms those traps into choices. Awareness removes manipulation. Consent becomes sacred again.

When you live by this understanding, relationships improve. You begin to respect the consent of others. You ask before assuming. You inform before requesting. Honour grows naturally because you now know its foundation. Every true relationship, whether personal or commercial, depends on mutual consent. Without it, even kindness becomes control.

Consent is not a weapon but a measure of respect. When councils act without consent, they betray their own stated purpose. They claim to serve community yet ignore the agreement of individuals. The Sovereign response is not anger but education. Each notice you send teaches that consent matters. Each question you ask invites others to remember what they have forgotten.

Silence has spiritual significance as well as practical power. In the presence of truth, silence expresses understanding. In the presence of deceit, silence appears as agreement. The difference lies in intent. The Sovereign uses silence consciously. They choose when to speak and when to remain still. That choice transforms silence from weakness into mastery.

To apply these principles, begin by examining all current obligations in your life. Identify where you have given consent through habit. Decide which agreements you wish to maintain and which you wish to withdraw. Serve notices where necessary. Keep copies of every communication. Over time, you will see a pattern. Life becomes lighter because assumption no longer burdens you.

Remember that withdrawal of consent must always be peaceful. Aggression invites retaliation. Calm withdrawal leaves no conflict. A simple statement of fact is enough: "I do not consent to this arrangement and require proof of lawful obligation." Such language holds power because it is true. It needs no defence or explanation. Truth stands quietly while falsehood collapses under noise.

The system's survival depends on your silence. Once you begin to communicate lawfully, the system loses certainty. It must either answer truthfully or reveal its deception through avoidance. Both outcomes serve awareness. Each letter you write weakens the foundation of presumption. Each question you ask restores the principle of consent to its rightful place.

The next section will explore how this understanding leads to the practice of conditional acceptance. You will learn how to use notice to turn offers into evidence, how to respond to demands without aggression, and how to make peace your strongest reply.

Silence is often described as golden, yet its value depends on how it is used. When silence comes from awareness, it expresses strength. When it comes from fear or apathy, it becomes surrender. In law and commerce, silence always carries meaning. The system interprets every lack of reply as agreement because unchallenged words stand as truth. Understanding this principle is vital to living lawfully.

A lawful society functions through communication. Notice, response, and resolution are its rhythm. When any part of that rhythm is broken, confusion arises. The system takes advantage of that confusion by defining silence as consent. When a man or woman fails to answer a claim, the claim stands unrebutted. It becomes accepted fact. That is why you must always answer, even if your answer is only a question. Your silence strengthens the system's presumption. Your written word dissolves it.

Every notice you send restores balance between consent and authority. It reminds those in office that consent cannot be assumed. When you write, you reclaim control of communication. You become equal participant in dialogue rather than silent subject of command. This equality is the essence of lawful exchange.

When councils issue demands, they expect silence. They are trained to interpret it as acceptance. This expectation allows them to move swiftly from notice to enforcement. The moment you reply, the process slows. The system must consider your questions, even if it refuses to answer them. Your letter becomes evidence that the claim is disputed. Enforcement without resolution becomes dishonour. This is how lawful correspondence protects you.

Some believe that ignoring letters from councils will make the problem disappear. It does not. It strengthens the assumption of debt. The system records silence as agreement and continues as if proof were given. Ignoring deception allows it to grow. Confronting it calmly ends it. That is why every Sovereign responds, even when response feels uncomfortable. Each letter written in truth transforms fear into strength.

You may notice that official letters often demand response within a short period. These time limits are tools of control, not measures of fairness. True law allows reasonable time for consideration. When a letter imposes a deadline without consent, it is invitation to contract under duress. You are free to reject such pressure by replying in your own time with clarity. The key is not speed but precision. A thoughtful reply holds more power than a hasty one.

Silence also plays a role in personal conduct. There will be moments when others attempt to provoke reaction. In those moments, silence is wisdom. You must know when to speak and when to remain still. Words have power. Use them only when they serve peace. Silence used with intent is message of its own. It says, "I will not engage in conflict." That kind of silence restores dignity.

Consent has another dimension rarely understood. It must remain continuous. Agreement given once can be withdrawn if circumstances change. Many assume that signing a form or registering property creates permanent obligation. It does not. Consent exists only while awareness remains. You have the right to withdraw consent at any time, provided you do so without deceit. Councils rely on ignorance of this right. When you remind them that consent is ongoing choice, their authority weakens.

To withdraw consent properly, issue written notice. State that you no longer consent to the arrangement or presumption. Include the reason briefly and end with peace. Keep a copy for your record and ensure delivery can be proven. This action closes the door of assumption. Future claims based on past consent become invalid. The record shows that you acted lawfully and in honour.

Understanding the power of consent also reveals the illusion of compulsory taxation. Councils claim that payment is mandatory, yet they never show the contract that created obligation. They depend on silence as proof. When enough people respond with lawful questions, the system must reveal its foundation or admit its absence. That admission marks the beginning of reform. Awareness always precedes change.

The same principle applies in wider society. Governments, corporations, and institutions all operate through consent. They function because the public agrees to play along. When individuals withdraw consent peacefully, the machinery loses energy. The withdrawal need not be loud or dramatic. A single letter, written in truth, changes the record forever. Silence after withdrawal holds new meaning. It no longer signals acceptance but completion.

Consent also connects deeply with honour. To give consent knowingly is act of honour. To act under assumption is act of ignorance. When you learn to give or withhold consent consciously, you restore honour to your life. Every choice becomes deliberate. Every agreement becomes sacred. You no longer blame others for your circumstances because you recognise your role in creating them. This self-awareness is the mark of the Sovereign.

You will find that councils and officials often avoid discussing consent directly. They prefer to speak of duty, policy, or regulation. These words distract from the central issue. Without consent, their authority is limited to those who identify as persons under statute. The living being operates under law, not policy. By maintaining this distinction in your correspondence, you reveal the truth that authority fears to face.

The law of consent is simple but profound. You have the right to choose, and you have the right to say no. You also have the duty to respect others' right to do the same. When society forgets this, control replaces cooperation. Councils act without consent because people let them. The remedy is education, not conflict. Teach through example. Show that peace and knowledge hold greater strength than protest.

Silence, when used correctly, becomes partner of truth. After you have written and served your notices, you may choose silence as final act. That silence declares completion. It says, "My record is complete. I have acted in honour." This form of silence carries authority because it follows action. It cannot be mistaken for consent because communication has already corrected assumption. This is the silence of peace.

In daily life, practise awareness of how often silence speaks for you. Notice when you remain quiet to avoid discomfort and when you remain quiet because truth requires no defence. The first weakens you. The second strengthens you. Each moment of choice teaches mastery.

The principle of consent and silence extends beyond correspondence. It shapes every aspect of existence. Relationships thrive when consent is mutual and silence is respected. Families remain peaceful when members act with awareness. Communities flourish when decisions are made through agreement, not force. Law begins in these small acts of fairness.

To live by consent is to live free. Freedom does not mean doing whatever you wish. It means acting without coercion. The man or woman who respects consent respects life itself. Councils and corporations lose power over such individuals because coercion no longer works. The Sovereign lives in peace not because the world has changed but because they have remembered choice.

When you combine consent with honour, silence with awareness, and peace with clarity, you become untouchable by deceit. No system can enslave a mind that understands its own authority. Each written word, each act of calm awareness, becomes part of a greater restoration. The world slowly adjusts to match the level of consciousness within it.

The next chapter will build upon these principles by exploring how to read official notices and summonses as commercial offers. You will learn how to identify hidden terms, recognise the language of assumption, and respond with honour. Once you see every letter as invitation rather than command, fear disappears, and peace takes its place.

Chapter 5:
Reading the Summons as a Commercial Offer

A summons is the most feared document in the council tax process. For many, it represents finality, proof that authority has triumphed. People see the word and imagine judges, police, and punishment. Yet the truth is far simpler. The council tax summons is not a command of law. It is a commercial offer presented in the form of authority. Once you understand its nature, fear vanishes.

A summons is meant to invite appearance. It is a request to attend a hearing so that matters of account can be discussed. It is not a lawful order issued under common law jurisdiction. It is an administrative notice sent under statute, addressed to the legal persona, not the living being. The power it holds depends entirely on belief. Without belief, it becomes paper carrying offer rather than command.

When you receive a summons, the first step is to observe without reaction. Do not allow emotion to lead. Read it as you would any letter from a company. Identify who sent it, who signed it, and what evidence it presents. You will notice that the document is rarely signed by any living man or woman taking responsibility. It bears the printed name of the council or court but lacks verifiable signature. In law, an unsigned document cannot impose obligation. It is proposal, not judgment.

The wording of a summons reveals its commercial nature. Phrases such as "you are hereby required to attend" or "failure to appear may result in further costs" are crafted to create compliance through fear. Yet nowhere does it explain the origin of obligation. It cites statutes but never contract. It demands payment but never proves agreement. The form imitates law while lacking its substance.

Councils issue summonses in bulk. Hundreds of names are processed at once. The so-called court hearing is administrative session designed for efficiency, not justice. The clerk or magistrate reads from prepared list, approving liability orders without examining individual cases. This process would be unlawful under true law, which demands evidence and hearing of both sides. In the commercial system, efficiency replaces fairness. The illusion of law hides a revenue procedure.

To expose this illusion, approach the summons as an offer of contract. The council, acting as corporate entity, is proposing that you attend a meeting to settle an account. You have three choices. You can accept, reject, or conditionally accept. Acceptance confirms liability. Rejection may appear dishonourable if expressed in hostility. Conditional acceptance, however, places you in peace while demanding proof. You may write, "I am willing to attend and settle any lawful obligation upon proof of claim." This simple statement turns the offer back on the sender. It removes assumption and restores equality.

Conditional acceptance is powerful because it neither denies nor agrees. It transforms accusation into dialogue. By requiring evidence of contract, you force the council to disclose the foundation of its claim. In most cases, they cannot. Their silence or avoidance becomes record of dishonour. You have not refused to pay. You have asked to see proof that payment is owed. No lawful system can punish that request.

Many people believe they must attend court when summoned. Attendance is voluntary unless proven otherwise by signed order of a judge in a court of record. Council tax hearings take place in administrative settings, not courts of record. No jury sits. No oath is taken. No independent record of evidence exists. These are the marks of commerce, not law. The choice to attend should be made consciously, not through fear.

If you decide to attend, do so as observer, not as defendant. When your name is called, stand calmly and say, "I am here to settle any lawful obligation upon proof of claim." Speak clearly, without aggression. The clerk may appear confused because the words do not fit expected script. You are not there to argue. You are there to offer peace through truth. If they proceed without addressing your question, you have witnessed dishonour. Record everything.

In many cases, councils withdraw before the hearing or after receiving your written reply. They know that their process cannot withstand scrutiny. It is easier for them to focus on silent compliance than on informed challenge. Your correspondence removes profit from presumption. When dishonour costs more than truth, the system chooses silence.

Examine the summons carefully. It often includes phrases such as "liability order to be applied for." The use of future tense is important. It shows that no order yet exists. The letter itself is proposal, not outcome. The liability order, once granted, functions as internal authorisation for enforcement. It is not judicial decision in lawful sense. Understanding this removes its power. It becomes internal paperwork of a corporation, not sentence of court.

Another clue lies in the use of language. The summons refers to "defendant" and "offence," terms borrowed from criminal law to create fear. Yet council tax is civil matter based on statute, not crime based on harm. The use of criminal terminology is deliberate manipulation. It encourages emotional submission. When you recognise this, you read with calm eyes. You see commercial offer hidden within theatrical costume of law.

When replying to a summons, remain polite and factual. Address your letter to the named officer or department. Acknowledge receipt and express willingness to resolve any lawful claim. Then request the following information:

1. Proof that a lawful contract exists between the council and the living man or woman.
2. Evidence that you consented to be bound by the statutes cited.
3. Identification of the living claimant taking responsibility for the demand.

4. Confirmation that the hearing will take place in a court of record under oath.

End your letter with statement of peace such as, "This communication is made in honour and with goodwill." Keep a copy in your private archive. This record protects you. It proves that you acted lawfully and sought truth.

If the council or court replies without addressing your points, you may send a notice of fault and opportunity to cure. This notice reminds them that their failure to provide evidence constitutes dishonour. You give reasonable time for correction. If silence continues, you may issue a decree of closure declaring the matter settled in peace. Each step follows lawful order. Notice, opportunity, decree. This rhythm maintains honour and creates unbreakable record.

Reading the summons as commercial offer reveals that power lies not in paper but in perception. The same letter that terrifies one person empowers another. Fear arises from ignorance. Knowledge turns fear into curiosity. You begin to read differently. You look beyond tone to content. You ask, "Where is the signature? Where is the evidence? Who takes responsibility?" Each unanswered question increases your understanding.

The council's entire authority rests on the belief that a summons equals law. Once that belief fades, the structure weakens. The man or woman who responds lawfully becomes mirror to the system. The reflection shows absence of conscience behind policy. Some officials will quietly recognise this truth and retreat. Others will double down in confusion. Your task is not to change them but to remain calm. Peace outlasts fear.

The summons is test of self-awareness. It asks whether you will act as person or as living being. The person reacts, panics, and obeys. The living being observes, writes, and remains still. The difference is not in status but in consciousness. Both receive the same letter. Only one reads it correctly.

To master this stage, you must control language. Never deny receipt. Acknowledge the document as offer. Never argue about law. Ask for evidence of obligation. Never claim immunity. State willingness to act in honour. These simple rules protect you. They transform interaction from conflict to education. Each letter you send teaches the system that honour still exists.

The next section will deepen this practice by explaining how to craft and use conditional acceptance as lawful reply. You will learn how to turn every demand into opportunity for proof, how to write with authority, and how to maintain peace while standing firm. Once you master conditional acceptance, you will hold the key to lawful dialogue with any institution.

A summons may look final, but in truth it marks the beginning of dialogue. The document itself carries no lawful power until accepted. When you see it as an invitation rather than command, fear turns into clarity. Each sentence becomes part of an offer waiting for your response. The more calmly you read, the clearer the deception becomes.

The structure of a summons follows the pattern of commercial correspondence. It begins with identification of parties, includes an account number, lists an amount claimed, and states time and place for response. These are the elements of offer. The sender presents terms, expecting acceptance either through payment or appearance. The words appear strong, yet their strength ends at your consent. Without it, the summons remains proposal on paper.

Every summons includes reference to statutes that appear to grant authority. Yet no statute can bind a living being without agreement. The council cannot prove that you consented to the Local Government Finance Act or any other policy. They rely on silence as evidence. Once you answer with lawful questions, the presumption of consent disappears. You shift the matter from assumption to accountability.

It is important to separate form from content. The form looks official. It may bear a court crest, reference number, and stern language. Yet form alone does not create law. A crown printed on paper is decoration. True law requires verified claim and accountable claimant. Without both, authority is fiction.

When you receive such a document, treat it as lesson rather than threat. The first question to ask is, who is making the claim? The second is, where is the evidence of obligation? The third is, what law requires performance? These questions expose the emptiness behind the form. Bureaucracy cannot answer them without revealing its commercial nature.

Some councils attempt to legitimise the process by including a note stating that the summons has been issued by the magistrates' court. Yet in practice, it is generated electronically by council staff. No magistrate reads or signs each case. The council's computer system produces lists that the court clerk approves in bulk. This practice demonstrates the administrative, not judicial, character of the proceedings. Once you know this, the illusion of personal judgment disappears.

The use of court names and symbols in council correspondence serves psychological purpose. People associate those symbols with justice and power. They obey instinctively. The council's process depends on that reflex. Awareness removes it. You learn to look beyond appearance. A printed crest cannot override truth. Authority begins in the conscience of the living, not in the design of a letterhead.

Reading a summons as commercial offer teaches you to identify layers of assumption. The council assumes you are the legal person. It assumes you consented to statute. It assumes you accepted benefit by occupying property. Each assumption must be proven to become lawful. Conditional acceptance removes assumption by demanding proof. It transforms the summons into opportunity for transparency.

A well-written conditional acceptance should follow the rhythm of honour. Begin by acknowledging receipt of the document. State your intention to settle any lawful obligation upon proof of claim. Then request the evidence required to confirm the validity of the offer. These questions might include:

1. Evidence that a lawful contract exists between the parties.
2. Proof that you consented to be bound by the cited statutes.
3. Identification of the living claimant responsible for the demand.

4. Clarification of whether the hearing will be held in a court of record under oath.

Each question targets a specific assumption. Together they shift burden of proof to the council. End your letter with affirmation of peace. A phrase such as "I write in honour and with goodwill" closes the communication on firm ground. Always keep a copy and proof of delivery.

Conditional acceptance turns the summons into instrument of learning. It invites the other party to operate in truth. Those who act without evidence will avoid response. Their silence becomes admission of error. Those who act with integrity will answer directly. Either outcome clarifies reality. The process is never about victory. It is about exposure of truth.

You may wonder whether failure to attend court after sending such notice carries risk. In commercial terms, the only risk is assumption of default. However, your record protects you. Your letters show willingness to engage and request for proof. No lawful system can condemn a man or woman for asking questions. If a liability order is still issued, it carries no moral or lawful weight because the foundation remains unproven. The paper exists, but the truth does not.

Some choose to attend hearings to witness the process firsthand. If you do, maintain the same calm approach. Speak only when necessary. Identify yourself as living man or woman appearing to settle any lawful claim upon proof of obligation. Avoid argument. Ask questions clearly and respectfully. Record the proceedings if allowed. Remember that your presence serves education, not confrontation.

The atmosphere in such hearings often reveals the nature of the system. The process moves quickly, and many participants appear confused. Officials expect compliance. When someone speaks calmly and demands proof, they disrupt the flow. The clerk may attempt to silence you or move to next case. Remain composed. Their avoidance confirms your point. You have witnessed assumption replacing justice.

Always remember that peace is your protection. Anger invites control. Fear invites submission. Peace leaves no opening. The summons has power only when it creates reaction. When you act from stillness, its spell breaks. The system cannot proceed easily against one who understands.

After the process, regardless of outcome, write a notice of closure. State that you have seen no evidence of lawful obligation and that you hold no ill will. File it with your other records. Closure prevents lingering fear or resentment. Each completed process becomes part of your education. The more you engage with awareness, the less intimidation affects you.

Reading the summons as commercial offer also changes how you view communication in general. You begin to see every letter, form, or statement from authority as offer. Some offers serve fairness and deserve acceptance. Others serve control and deserve conditional acceptance or polite decline. This awareness restores choice. You no longer live by reaction but by decision.

The process described here is simple but powerful. It removes emotion from administration. It turns fear into enquiry. It restores equality through honour. Each time you read a summons without fear, you prove that peace is stronger than threat.

In time, your understanding influences others. Friends, family, and colleagues may notice your calmness and ask why you are untroubled by official letters. You can explain gently that authority functions by consent and that peace holds greater force than protest. Share knowledge without pride. True education spreads quietly through example.

The council tax summons is symbol of wider issue. It represents how society has replaced consent with compliance. Learning to read it correctly teaches you how to live freely in all areas. It shows that every apparent order is invitation in disguise. Freedom begins not with rebellion but with comprehension.

The next chapter will expand on this understanding by explaining how to use conditional acceptance as structured process. You will learn how to write clearly, set lawful conditions, and maintain tone of peace. When you master that skill, every demand becomes opportunity for honourable dialogue, and no letter will ever frighten you again.

Chapter 6:

Conditional Acceptance for Proof of Obligation

Conditional acceptance is the bridge between peace and power. It allows you to answer any demand without conflict and without submission. It is the tool that transforms fear into communication. Where most people react to authority with either silence or anger, the Sovereign responds with reason. Conditional acceptance embodies that reason in written form. It stands as statement of truth and act of honour.

The phrase itself is simple. To accept conditionally means to agree subject to proof. It says, "I am willing to settle any lawful obligation upon evidence that one exists." Those few words change the entire relationship between you and the claimant. They remove assumption and create balance. You do not refuse the offer. You do not agree to it blindly. You ask for proof. Law respects those who act with honour. Dishonour arises only when you refuse without reason or accept without understanding. Conditional acceptance rests perfectly between those extremes.

The process begins when you receive a letter demanding payment or compliance. Rather than ignore or argue, you write your reply. Your first sentence should always acknowledge receipt. This shows that you act in good faith. The next sentence should express your willingness to settle any lawful obligation upon proof of claim. Then you list your conditions. These usually include requests for evidence of contract, proof of consent, and identification of the living claimant. End the letter by affirming that your communication is made in peace and honour.

The tone of conditional acceptance must always remain calm. Anger weakens authority because it shows uncertainty. Confidence in truth requires no aggression. The council employee reading your letter may never have encountered such correspondence before. They may be confused or defensive. Your task is not to provoke but to educate. The spirit of conditional acceptance is teaching through example. You are reminding others that law still lives in communication, not command.

Each condition you include serves a purpose. Requesting proof of contract exposes assumption of obligation. Asking for evidence of consent challenges the claim of authority. Demanding identification of the claimant removes the mask of office. These questions force the institution to face its own limitations. They cannot produce what does not exist. Silence or evasion that follows becomes your record of truth.

In commercial law, every claim must be verified by evidence. Without verification, it remains allegation. Councils operate by presumption because they know few people will ask for proof. The system depends on mass obedience, not individual understanding. Conditional acceptance reverses that dynamic. It places responsibility back on the claimant. It says politely, "Show me your authority, and I will comply." That is honour.

When drafting your notice, structure matters. Begin with date, your full name written as living man or woman, and address for correspondence. Clearly state that you are writing in response to their letter or demand, referencing its date and any account number. Then include your statement of conditional acceptance. Example: "I, a living man known as Roger of the family Davies, am willing to settle any lawful obligation upon proof of claim." Follow this with your specific conditions:

1. Proof that a valid contract exists bearing the signatures of both parties.
2. Evidence that consent was freely given without misrepresentation or duress.
3. Identification of the living man or woman making the claim and taking liability for its truth.

4. Confirmation that the matter will be heard in a court of record under oath if dispute arises.

These points form the foundation of honourable enquiry. They are reasonable, lawful, and clear. No honest system should fear them.

You should also include reasonable time for response, usually fourteen days. This demonstrates patience and fairness. Close with affirmation of peace: "This communication is made in good faith and honour." Sign with your living name, not the legal persona. Do not use titles such as Mr or Ms, as these refer to corporate identity. Simplicity carries strength.

Once written, send your letter by recorded delivery and keep all receipts. Place a copy in your private archive with reference number and date. Your archive is the foundation of your lawful record. It shows process, patience, and integrity. Each letter becomes evidence of your understanding. The system respects record even when it ignores conscience. When conscience and record unite, they become unbreakable.

The council may respond with standard letter avoiding your questions. This is common. They will restate statutes, repeat demand, or claim that they are under no obligation to answer. Their avoidance confirms dishonour. A lawful claimant always welcomes questions. When silence follows enquiry, deception stands exposed.

At that point, issue a notice of fault and opportunity to cure. This document reminds the council that they failed to provide requested proof and gives them set period to correct error. The notice may say: "You have failed to provide evidence of contract or consent as requested. This notice serves as opportunity to cure within ten days. Failure to respond will confirm absence of proof." Always maintain tone of peace. You are not threatening. You are documenting.

If silence continues after that, you may issue decree of closure. This final notice declares the matter resolved in peace due to absence of evidence. It may state: "Having given fair opportunity to provide proof and received none, I now close this matter in honour, holding no ill will." This step completes lawful process. It transforms presumption into truth through record.

Conditional acceptance requires discipline. You must resist the temptation to argue. Argument implies equality of confusion. Law requires clarity. Every letter should reflect that clarity. Short sentences carry more power than long explanations. Each word should serve purpose. Avoid emotional or accusatory language. Let truth speak quietly through structure.

This practice teaches self-control as much as law. When you write with peace, you train your mind to separate emotion from reason. You begin to see correspondence not as battle but as reflection. The letters you send mirror your level of awareness. If you write in fear, fear returns. If you write in honour, peace returns. The process itself becomes spiritual training.

Conditional acceptance also applies beyond council tax. It can be used in any situation where demand appears without proof. Whether it is letter from bank, agency, or court, the principle remains. Accept conditionally upon proof. This approach never fails because truth never fears examination.

The power of this method lies in its balance. It rejects nothing and accepts nothing blindly. It places burden of proof where it belongs, on the claimant. In doing so, it reveals character of both parties. The one who acts in honour provides evidence. The one who acts in deceit hides behind authority. Either way, truth emerges.

Some worry that conditional acceptance may appear confrontational. It is not. It is highest form of courtesy in law. It says, "I take your words seriously enough to examine them." That level of respect disarms hostility. It transforms transaction into conversation. Many officials are unaccustomed to such treatment. They expect aggression or submission, not honour. When you respond differently, they notice.

The process also creates space for self-reflection. Before challenging any demand, ask yourself whether the obligation may in fact be lawful. If evidence exists and you knowingly owe, honour demands that you fulfil it. The goal is not avoidance but balance. Conditional acceptance is tool for truth, not escape. It protects against deception while preserving integrity.

The living being who practises conditional acceptance becomes student of patience. You learn to wait for silence, to observe rather than react, and to act only when record demands it. Each step builds inner peace. You stop fearing letters because you know how to answer them. You stop fearing systems because you know their limits. That confidence is freedom in action.

The next section will provide examples of how to apply conditional acceptance specifically to council tax demands. You will learn how to write, serve, and record your notices so that they remain unassailable in both conscience and law. When used properly, conditional acceptance turns every demand into lesson in peace and every letter into evidence of truth.

Conditional acceptance functions best when approached as peaceful dialogue rather than defence. It reminds both sides that law exists to bring understanding, not domination. The council may attempt to interpret your notice as refusal to pay, but that is misunderstanding. Your words make clear that you are willing to fulfil any lawful duty. You simply require evidence that such duty exists. That distinction separates law from coercion.

When councils receive conditional acceptance, they often reply with automated letters that repeat statute and policy. These replies prove nothing. They avoid your questions and attempt to regain control through repetition. In such cases, you must stay calm and respond only once more. Repeat your conditions, remind them of the unanswered points, and give specific period for remedy. There is no need to engage endlessly. One clear reminder followed by silence on their part completes the record.

The strength of conditional acceptance lies in rhythm. Notice, opportunity, closure. Each step must follow naturally. You cannot skip the offer of remedy because honour requires fairness. Nor can you delay closure once the period has passed. Discipline of timing shows integrity. It also proves that your communication is process, not argument. Law respects process. Bureaucracy respects repetition. When you master both, you are untouchable by deceit.

It is also important to understand the emotional aspect. The system uses language designed to unsettle. Demands may threaten legal action, court costs, or enforcement. These phrases are meant to trigger fear, which overrides logic. Conditional acceptance neutralises this by replacing emotion with structure. Once you follow clear steps, fear loses ground. You know what to do, when to do it, and why. That knowledge restores calm.

The key to mastery is preparation. Keep templates of your notices ready, but adapt each one to the specific situation. Never copy blindly. Authenticity carries energy that formality cannot imitate. When you write, imagine speaking directly to the living being behind the desk. Address them with respect. Honour opens more doors than force ever will.

One of the most powerful effects of conditional acceptance is educational. Every letter you send becomes seed of awareness planted within the system. Some officials begin to question why they cannot provide the proof you request. They may research quietly and discover the limits of their authority. You may never know the results, but truth spreads silently. The act of asking questions transforms both sender and receiver.

Conditional acceptance also reinforces your understanding of contract. You begin to recognise that all interaction between institutions and individuals follows commercial pattern. Offers, acceptances, and consideration form hidden structure of society. Once you see this, you can navigate every exchange consciously. You stop signing thoughtlessly or agreeing impulsively. Each act becomes deliberate. This discipline extends beyond paperwork into every decision you make.

A well-documented process of conditional acceptance protects you even years later. Should any dispute arise, your archive serves as shield. It shows that you acted in good faith and sought resolution through peace. No reasonable tribunal could condemn such behaviour. Record is your silent witness. Keep it organised. Store both digital and physical copies. Index each document with dates, subjects, and outcomes. Order reflects clarity, and clarity reflects law.

There are common mistakes to avoid. The first is adding unnecessary arguments about legality or conspiracy. These weaken focus and invite dismissal. Keep communication factual. The second is using aggressive language. Words of threat or insult destroy honour and give the system excuse to ignore you. The third is impatience. Honourable process takes time. Expect silence. Treat it as confirmation, not rejection.

You will find that once you have served two or three cycles of notice, your confidence grows. You stop seeing letters from councils as threats. They become opportunities to practise discipline. The process becomes routine act of peace. Each time you act with honour, your inner authority strengthens. External authority loses control because it no longer controls your emotion.

Conditional acceptance is not merely a strategy for correspondence. It is philosophy of life. It teaches balance between courage and humility. It reminds you that truth does not need defence, only expression. The one who accepts conditionally stands between aggression and submission. They neither fight nor flee. They stand. This posture is foundation of sovereignty.

When dealing specifically with council tax, remember that each demand follows commercial structure. The first bill is offer. The reminder is second offer. The summons is final offer disguised as command. Conditional acceptance meets each stage with peace. You acknowledge receipt, express willingness to settle, and request proof. Once silence confirms absence of proof, you close record. The system moves on to easier targets. Peace replaces fear because you know procedure.

You may encounter collection agencies claiming to act on behalf of the council. Their letters are continuation of same offer. Respond with same calm structure. Ask for proof that debt exists, proof that they purchased it lawfully, and proof that contract binds you. They will rarely reply substantively because they cannot. Their business model depends on assumption. When assumption meets awareness, it collapses quietly.

Conditional acceptance also harmonises with natural law. In nature, balance arises through mutual recognition. Every action carries equal reaction. When you accept conditionally, you acknowledge the offer while maintaining equality. You do not dominate or submit. You mirror truth. This alignment with natural balance is why the process feels peaceful. It restores harmony even within artificial systems.

As your understanding deepens, conditional acceptance becomes instinct. You no longer need to consult notes. The words form naturally because they reflect truth. This instinct will guide you not only in written communication but also in daily conversation. When confronted with unreasonable demand, you will respond, "I am willing to consider that upon proof." Those words disarm aggression and restore fairness instantly.

The ultimate purpose of conditional acceptance is not victory over councils but education of self. It trains you to think clearly, to act deliberately, and to remain peaceful under pressure. These qualities extend beyond law into every part of life. The more you practise, the more authority loses its hold. The system depends on reaction. You have replaced reaction with reflection.

Conditional acceptance also honours those who act lawfully. If you receive genuine evidence of obligation, fulfil it promptly. Honour does not hide behind technicality. It fulfils truth wherever found. This balance keeps your conscience clear and your record strong. The goal is not to escape duty but to ensure that duty arises from truth.

The final step in conditional acceptance is closure through forgiveness. Once the process ends, release all resentment. Do not dwell on unfairness or delay. The energy of anger ties you to the very system you seek to transcend. Closure restores freedom of mind. You have acted in truth. That is enough.

The next chapter will explain how jurisdiction operates in council proceedings and how understanding joinder protects you from assumption of liability. You will learn how presence, signature, and language create or remove jurisdiction, and how to remain in peace while asserting your living status. With that knowledge, you will complete the foundation for full lawful communication.

Chapter 7:
Jurisdiction Challenges in Council Courts

Jurisdiction is the boundary of authority. Without it, no court, council, or officer can act lawfully. The word itself means "to speak the law." For that speech to have effect, both parties must agree that the speaker has authority to speak. Without consent, jurisdiction is assumption dressed as law. Understanding this principle is essential when dealing with council tax proceedings.

Council courts are not courts of law. They are administrative forums created to process paperwork under statute. Their function is financial, not judicial. They exist to confirm liability orders, not to test truth. The proceedings are designed for speed and volume. Each case lasts only minutes. Hundreds are processed in single morning. Such setting cannot produce justice. It can only confirm assumption.

The man or woman who enters such room believing it to be court of law places themselves under its authority. That act of belief creates joinder. Joinder occurs when the living being connects with the legal persona named on the papers. Once joinder occurs, the court assumes jurisdiction. From that moment, everything said or done within the room operates under statute. The remedy lies in preventing that joinder through awareness.

When you receive summons, you are invited to create jurisdiction by appearance. If you attend without challenge, the invitation becomes acceptance. The system depends on that silent agreement. The simple act of stepping into the room confirms consent. Yet no law compels you to appear in administrative hearing that lacks lawful foundation. Attendance is voluntary unless order bearing signature of judge of record exists. Councils rarely possess such order.

If you choose to attend, your awareness becomes shield. Jurisdiction requires clear identification of the parties and the subject matter. You are not the corporate name printed in capital letters. That name represents legal fiction created by registration. You are the living man or woman who can speak for yourself. When your name is called, stand calmly and say, "I am here by special appearance to settle any lawful obligation upon proof of claim." Those words preserve your standing under law while denying assumption of personhood.

Special appearance is ancient principle of law. It allows a man or woman to enter a court only to question its authority, not to submit to it. Once you declare special appearance, the tribunal must first prove jurisdiction before proceeding. In true courts, this process is respected. In council hearings, it is often ignored. The clerks are trained to continue regardless. Their behaviour does not change the fact that jurisdiction remains unproven. Record your words and actions. They form evidence of dishonour.

If asked to confirm your name or address, reply carefully. Do not say, "Yes, that is me." That statement joins you with the legal persona. Instead, you may say, "That is a name I use." This phrase acknowledges the name as tool of identification without surrendering your living status. Authority depends on consent through language. Precision protects you.

Jurisdiction also depends on subject matter. The court must have authority over the type of dispute presented. Council tax arises from statute, not law. Administrative courts exist to enforce statute, not to judge conscience. When you stand as living being, you operate under law, not statute. The two jurisdictions are distinct. Without voluntary transition, the court cannot bridge them.

In correspondence, you can challenge jurisdiction by requesting proof that the court is court of record. A true court of record requires independent judge, jury, and record of evidence. Council hearings lack all three. They are offices of administration, not courts of justice. Asking for clarification exposes this difference. Silence or refusal to answer confirms absence of lawful jurisdiction.

Many people fear questioning authority in such settings. They believe that judges or clerks hold ultimate power. In truth, they hold position of trust, not dominion. Their authority extends only as far as consent allows. The living being who speaks calmly from truth cannot be forced to contract. Threats may occur, but they carry no lawful weight. Fear creates submission. Knowledge creates peace.

Jurisdiction also operates through energy of words. When you enter court in anger, you strengthen its power because anger signals belief in its authority. When you enter in peace, the system loses energy. Its language becomes noise rather than command. This is why maintaining composure matters. Peace removes fuel from deception.

One of the simplest ways to challenge jurisdiction is to ask, "Do you have verified claim against me, and is this a court of record under oath?" If no answer comes, you may say, "Without verified claim and court of record, I see no jurisdiction." Then remain silent. You have stated truth. Further argument is unnecessary. Those who act in ignorance may continue procedure, but their record reveals dishonour.

You may hear the phrase "liability order granted." In truth, no judicial order is issued. The phrase describes internal authorisation for enforcement. It is administrative, not lawful. The so-called order is printed later without signature or record of evidence. Once you understand this, fear of the term disappears. It is bookkeeping, not judgment.

The idea of jurisdiction also extends to enforcement. When bailiffs or agents act under council authority, they rely on same presumed order. You may ask them to show signed warrant bearing name of judge of record. They will not have one. Their papers cite regulation, not law. Without lawful warrant, their presence is trespass. Respond with calm notice, not confrontation. Ask for proof and record interaction.

Awareness of jurisdiction transforms how you view all institutions. You begin to see that authority exists only where consent meets honour. Every court, office, or agency operates within limited field defined by agreement. When officials exceed those limits, they act personally. The living being who understands this never feels powerless again.

Jurisdiction cannot be taken. It can only be given. Councils and courts cannot force you to believe. They can only persuade. Their power lies in persuasion through fear. Your power lies in peace through knowledge. Once you know the difference, you step beyond reach of deception.

In true law, jurisdiction arises from truth, harm, and evidence. When no harm exists, no court has cause to act. Council tax involves no harmed party, only unpaid claim by corporation. This is commercial matter requiring contract. Without proof of contract, no lawful cause exists. The council's claim belongs to commerce, not justice. You may remind them of this politely in writing.

Always remember that jurisdiction follows the living being. Wherever you stand in truth, law stands with you. No building or title can add to or remove that fact. The purpose of this chapter is not to create defiance but to restore understanding. You do not fight courts. You remind them of their boundaries.

The next section will explore how jurisdiction and joinder relate directly to the concept of the strawman. You will learn how councils use the legal persona to attach liability and how to respond in honour without conflict. Once you grasp that connection, you will understand why paperwork, names, and signatures hold such power and how to reclaim that power peacefully.

Jurisdiction determines whether a court's words carry weight or merely sound. Without it, all proceedings become theatre. Councils and administrative courts rely on the public not knowing this. They use appearance, uniform, and ritual to project power. Yet every one of those symbols depends on consent. If consent is withdrawn, the structure loses foundation.

The greatest misunderstanding is that jurisdiction is absolute. It is not. It must be proven for each case. No court, however grand, possesses automatic authority over a living man or woman. Authority must be granted through contract, oath, or consent. When you do not grant it, jurisdiction cannot exist. Those who act without it commit fraud by assumption.

The process of assumption begins long before any hearing. When you register a birth, a legal persona is created. That persona exists as corporate entity attached to your name in capital letters. Councils and courts interact with that persona, not with you as living being. The summons, the bill, and the judgment all refer to that paper entity. The living man or woman unknowingly answers for it, creating joinder. That single act brings them under jurisdiction. The remedy lies in awareness of the distinction.

When corresponding with councils or attending hearings, always make the difference between person and living being clear. Write or state, "I am the living man known as Roger of the family Davies." This language separates you from corporate identity. It prevents automatic joinder and limits the reach of administrative jurisdiction. The words themselves carry power because they describe truth.

Jurisdiction is also created through signature. When you sign a document without understanding its implications, you give consent to its terms. Councils rely on this. Many forms, registrations, and declarations contain hidden clauses binding you to policy. Always read carefully. If you must sign, do so conditionally. Add the words "All rights reserved" or "Without prejudice." These phrases preserve sovereignty while acknowledging receipt. They prevent your signature being used as tool of consent.

The act of speaking also creates jurisdiction. Every word spoken in court is recorded as statement of the person. When you answer to the name, you become that person in law. The trick is simple but effective. The clerk calls, "Mr Davies." The living man stands and replies, "Yes." In that moment, joinder occurs. The system gains authority. To remain outside jurisdiction, do not answer to title. Respond instead, "I am here by special appearance and do not consent to being identified as that name." Speak calmly. The record will show that consent was not given.

You must also understand the difference between de jure and de facto courts. De jure means lawful, established by truth and consent. De facto means existing in fact but without lawful authority. Most modern courts, including those used for council tax, are de facto. They function because people believe they are lawful. Belief sustains them. Knowledge dissolves them. When you recognise a de facto court, treat it with respect but not fear. You stand above it in jurisdiction because you operate under law.

Officials may try to pressure you by claiming that failure to obey results in penalty. Ask them to show lawful proof that their rules apply to living beings. They cannot. They may show statute but never contract. Remember that statute governs persons, not men and women. Without joinder, statute cannot reach you. This understanding turns every threat into invitation for proof.

Jurisdiction also connects with the concept of capacity. A man or woman may appear in various capacities, such as trustee, agent, or beneficiary. Each capacity carries specific rights and duties. Councils assume you act as trustee for the legal persona created at birth. That presumption allows them to attach liability to you. You may correct this by declaring, "I appear as the living man and beneficiary, not as trustee or agent." This statement reverses assumption and reclaims control of the relationship.

You are not required to deny everything the court says. Denial invites argument. Silence in peace carries greater force. Once you have stated lack of consent, you need not repeat it. Each further statement risks drawing you into jurisdiction. The principle is simple: speak once, stand firm, stay silent. Let the record show that you did not agree.

When faced with intimidation, remember that courts exist to serve, not to rule. Their purpose is resolution of disputes, not creation of fear. The moment they step beyond that purpose, they lose legitimacy. Keep your focus on principle, not personality. The clerk, judge, or officer is human being caught in system of assumption. Treat them as such. Compassion disarms hostility.

Should you receive document claiming to be liability order or warrant, examine it carefully. A lawful warrant must bear signature of judge of record and wet seal of court. Most council documents contain only printed names. These are not signatures in law. They are administrative marks used for convenience. Without verified signature, no lawful authority exists. This simple fact reveals how much of the system operates on bluff.

It is wise to keep written record of every interaction. Send all correspondence by recorded delivery. Note times, dates, and names of anyone you speak with. If you attend hearing, make written record immediately afterwards. Your notes become evidence. In law, the one who keeps record holds truth. Councils rely on people forgetting or failing to document. Discipline in record-keeping protects you.

The deeper meaning of jurisdiction lies within yourself. It represents the boundary between internal authority and external control. When you forget who you are, external forces claim power over you. When you remember, they retreat. This is not mystical concept but practical truth. Confidence rooted in understanding radiates peace that systems cannot penetrate.

Jurisdiction is never permanent. It can be withdrawn at any time. If you have previously consented to process unknowingly, you may correct record through notice. State that any previous assumption of consent was made in error and that you now withdraw it. Once served, that notice removes authority for future action. Always close with affirmation of peace. Correction, not confrontation, is the goal.

The real court exists within conscience. When you act in honour, you stand in your own jurisdiction. No external system can override it. Administrative courts may continue their rituals, but their words carry no truth against a peaceful mind. The outcome of their paperwork has meaning only when you accept it. Understanding this removes all fear.

The lesson of jurisdiction is simple yet profound. Authority operates through belief. Withdraw belief, and it falls silent. Councils, courts, and officers hold no power over the living being who remembers their own authority. Your task is not to destroy their system but to outgrow it. When you walk in peace, the false court loses interest because it cannot profit from calmness.

The next chapter will build upon this understanding by exploring the role of the strawman in liability. You will see how councils and governments use the legal fiction to attach debts to living beings and how to separate yourself from that fiction without rejecting society. Once you grasp that distinction fully, you will never again mistake paper identity for truth.

Chapter 8:
The Role of the Strawman in Liability

Every system of control requires a substitute for the living being. It cannot touch life directly, so it creates symbol. In modern governance, that symbol is the strawman. The strawman is the paper identity formed when a birth is registered. It is the legal persona that carries your name in capital letters. It has no breath, no conscience, and no soul. Yet through it, the system claims ownership of labour, property, and obedience. Understanding this creation is key to freeing yourself from presumed liability.

When a child is born, the parents sign a registration document. That act creates certificate, and with it, a corporate entity. The living child exists in flesh, but the registered name exists on paper. Two identities are now linked. One is real, the other symbolic. Governments, banks, and councils interact only with the symbol. They send letters, bills, and summonses to it. When you answer as if you are that symbol, you join yourself to its liabilities.

The strawman functions as intermediary between man and state. It allows commerce to operate without direct consent. Every contract, licence, and tax relies on the assumption that you act as representative of that entity. The council's demand for payment is addressed to the strawman, not to you. Yet when you open the letter and pay, you accept role of surety. You take responsibility for debt of artificial person. This is how liability is transferred from paper to flesh.

The language of government reveals this separation. Official letters refer to "person," "individual," or "citizen." None of these words describe living man or woman. They describe roles within system. A person is mask worn by actor. The term originates from Latin persona, meaning sound through, referring to mask used on stage. Law adopted this meaning. When you act as person, you speak through mask. The system recognises the mask, not the being behind it.

Councils issue demands to the mask. The envelope carries name in capital letters because corporations communicate only with other corporations. The living being is invisible to them. Their world is one of documents, not life. When you reply as living being rather than as mask, confusion arises. Their system cannot process consciousness. It expects compliance, not awareness.

The trick lies in language. When you say, "I am Mr Davies," you declare yourself legal person. When you say, "I am a man known as Roger of the family Davies," you speak as living being. The first statement joins you to the strawman. The second separates you from it. This difference seems small but holds enormous power. Law recognises distinction between name and being. The system depends on you forgetting it.

Liability attaches to the strawman because it is property of the state. The birth certificate proves registration, and registration means transfer of title. The state becomes trustee of the name. The living child becomes beneficiary but also surety for debts created in that name. Councils and agencies claim payment by sending bills to the registered entity. The man or woman who answers pays on behalf of creation they do not own.

The purpose of this knowledge is not to reject society but to restore balance. The strawman is useful tool when understood. It allows interaction with systems that cannot comprehend life. You may use it as interface while remembering you are not it. The problem arises only when you believe the mask is you. Then you become trapped within fiction, bound by statutes written for paper entities.

To free yourself from assumed liability, you must correct the record through notice. Declare that you are living man or woman and that you act as authorised agent for the name only when necessary. State that you do not consent to being treated as surety for debts of that name without written contract. Once served, this notice removes presumption. The council can no longer act as if you automatically guarantee obligations of strawman.

Some fear that separating from the strawman means abandoning rights or benefits. It does not. Rights belong to the living, not to paper. Benefits offered to the strawman are forms of control disguised as privilege. When you stand as living being, you may still choose to use certain services, but you do so by agreement, not by assumption. Freedom does not reject society. It redefines relationship between individual and system.

Understanding the strawman also explains why signatures matter. When you sign document using name of strawman, you authorise transaction within corporate world. If you sign unconsciously, you may accept liability without realising it. The solution is awareness. When you must sign, add statement preserving rights, such as "All rights reserved." This signals that you sign under protest or for limited purpose. It keeps boundary between living and paper intact.

Councils exploit ignorance of this process. They assume that by occupying property within their jurisdiction, you act as representative of strawman subject to statute. Yet no law compels living being to guarantee debts of corporate entity without consent. The moment you question this assumption, their authority falters. They cannot produce contract proving you accepted that role. Their silence becomes confession.

The strawman also plays role in court. When magistrate or clerk calls name, they are summoning paper entity. The moment you answer, you enter fiction. The court now holds jurisdiction over person, not over you. Awareness of this allows peaceful correction. You may say, "I am here concerning that matter but not as that name." The record then shows you did not accept role of strawman. This preserves your standing under law.

Many dismiss this understanding as theory because they cannot see paperwork's power. Yet the world runs on record. Banks, councils, and governments operate entirely through documentation. Whoever controls paper controls perception of truth. The living being who controls their own paper reclaims authority. Notice, affidavit, and declaration become tools of peace rather than rebellion.

To live free within system, you must learn to use its language without losing yourself in it. The strawman is mask. Wear it when needed, remove it when done. Do not destroy it, for destruction invites chaos. Mastery lies in use, not denial. You may use name to open account, travel, or communicate, while remaining aware that the name is not you. The mask serves you. You do not serve the mask.

This understanding transforms liability. When bill arrives addressed to name in capital letters, you recognise it as offer to strawman. You may choose to act as agent, request proof of contract, or decline politely. Each option remains yours. The system depends on belief in compulsion. Awareness reveals choice.

The next section will explore how to use this understanding in correspondence with councils. You will learn how to write notices that separate living being from paper identity, how to preserve peace while correcting record, and how to maintain authority without confrontation. Once mastered, this practice ends confusion and restores honour to every exchange.

To separate yourself from liability, you must learn how to communicate as the living being while acknowledging the existence of the strawman. Denying the name completely confuses the system and invites unnecessary conflict. Using it knowingly brings clarity. The name exists within corporate world as tool. You are not rejecting the tool, only defining its limits.

When writing to councils, use structure that reflects understanding. Begin by acknowledging receipt of their letter addressed to the name in capital letters. Then write, "I am the living man known as Roger of the family Davies, authorised agent for that name." This statement does three things. It confirms receipt, establishes living status, and clarifies relationship to the legal persona. From that position, you can communicate with confidence and peace.

Your notice should include declaration that you do not consent to being treated as surety for debts of registered name without written contract signed by both parties. Require evidence that such contract exists and that it was entered voluntarily with full disclosure. These requests are lawful and reasonable. Councils rarely reply with proof because none exists. Their silence forms record that they rely on presumption, not agreement.

This correspondence teaches council officers that there is difference between living being and legal fiction. Most have never considered it. They are trained to follow policy, not to question its foundation. When they encounter calm, factual notices, they face truth that procedure cannot explain. Some react defensively. Others begin to think differently. Your role is not to force awakening but to act consistently in honour. Truth spreads through example, not argument.

Always maintain peaceful tone. Anger reattaches you to fiction because it shows loss of control. The living being governs emotion. The strawman reacts. Each time you respond calmly, you prove distinction. This discipline protects you and strengthens your record. Law recognises calmness as mark of honour.

You may wish to include affidavit of living status within your correspondence. This is sworn statement declaring that you are living man or woman, not corporate entity. It can also state that you act as agent for registered name only by choice. Once signed, witnessed, and served, this affidavit stands as evidence in any dispute. It becomes your written proof of standing. Keep copy in your private archive.

The strawman's existence also explains how enforcement operates. When councils obtain liability orders, they direct them toward registered name. Enforcement agents act as if order applies to you personally, but in truth, it applies only to corporate entity. By reminding them of this distinction, you remove their foundation. Ask them to produce signed contract showing you accepted liability for that name. They will not have one. Their power ends where consent is denied.

It is wise to prepare notice specifically for enforcement situations. A short written statement can say, "I am the living man known as Roger of the family Davies. I do not consent to be treated as surety for debts of registered name. Please provide verified contract showing lawful obligation." Serve it calmly if approached. This single sheet removes assumption without confrontation. It shows awareness rather than resistance.

The concept of strawman also helps you understand why identification is always requested. Councils and agents ask for date of birth, postcode, or reference number because these details belong to corporate record. They seek confirmation that you accept role of strawman. When you provide them unconsciously, you strengthen connection. Awareness changes this. You can respond politely without confirming role. Example: "My correspondence is on record. Please refer to my previous notice." This keeps control while remaining respectful.

Freedom does not mean rejecting all identification. It means knowing how to use it. The living being uses tools of system while remaining master of them. The problem arises only when tools use the man. Every interaction becomes opportunity to practise balance. You choose when to act as agent and when to stand as living being. Both roles can exist in peace when boundaries are understood.

Councils depend on mass ignorance of these principles. The fewer people who know difference between living being and strawman, the stronger the illusion. Yet awareness is spreading. Each man or woman who learns acts as light within fog of confusion. Change never begins with crowds. It begins with individuals who remember truth.

Understanding the strawman also removes fear of paperwork. Once you realise that letters and demands are addressed to fiction, they lose emotional weight. You see them as business correspondence within corporate world, not moral judgments upon your soul. This realisation brings calm. Calmness is your greatest defence. Systems cannot feed on peace.

It is natural to question whether this understanding alone prevents enforcement. It does when combined with honourable communication. Councils may still send letters or agents, but without proof of contract, their actions rest on bluff. The living being who responds in writing with questions and keeps record holds advantage. The burden of proof remains with claimant. Silence on their part confirms nullity.

Remember that the strawman itself is not enemy. It is neutral creation used for commerce. The problem lies in deception that hides its nature. When you understand it, you can use it wisely. You can trade, travel, and work within system without surrendering freedom. The key is awareness. Awareness turns control into cooperation.

To maintain separation between you and strawman, avoid using titles unnecessarily. In private letters, omit "Mr," "Ms," or "Mrs." Use full name only when necessary for clarity. In legal matters, sign with statement of reservation such as "All rights reserved." These small habits accumulate. Each one reinforces boundary.

When speaking to officials, remain consistent. Do not switch between identities. If you act as agent, make it clear. If you speak as living being, maintain that stance. Consistency prevents confusion and strengthens record. Systems exploit inconsistency because it creates appearance of consent. Precision in language closes that door.

The understanding of strawman also changes perception of justice. You realise that courts do not judge living beings but manage accounts of corporate entities. Their task is administration, not morality. When you stop identifying with paper name, their judgments lose meaning. They can adjust accounts, but they cannot touch truth. This insight frees you from psychological chains of authority.

Ultimately, knowledge of strawman returns you to self-responsibility. Freedom carries duty. You become your own authority, your own court, and your own lawgiver. You decide what agreements to enter and which to decline. Councils lose power because you no longer act automatically. Every act becomes conscious. That consciousness is the true definition of sovereignty.

The next chapter will explore how to rebut assumptions of occupancy and benefit, two key presumptions used by councils to create liability. You will learn how to communicate clearly that use of property or services does not equal consent to taxation, and how to replace fear with peace through knowledge.

Chapter 9:

Rebutting Assumptions of Occupancy and Benefit

The modern system of council taxation rests on two silent presumptions. The first is the presumption of occupancy. The second is the presumption of benefit. Councils claim that because you live in property within their mapped boundary, you owe payment for services they provide. Yet at no point is contract shown, consent sought, or proof of benefit given. The process functions entirely on assumption. Understanding and rebutting these two pillars exposes the illusion of obligation.

The presumption of occupancy is straightforward. Councils assume that if you are registered at address or receive mail there, you are occupier. That assumption creates what they call liability. It sounds lawful but lacks foundation. Occupancy does not equal contract. To be liable, there must be agreement to terms, clear offer, and acceptance. No such agreement exists. You did not sign document consenting to pay for undefined services under threat of penalty. The council simply recorded your presence and converted it into account.

The presumption of benefit works in same way. The council claims that because you enjoy public lighting, waste collection, and other local functions, you have received benefit and therefore owe payment. Yet true benefit must be measurable, specific, and voluntary. If service is imposed without request, it cannot create lawful obligation. Benefit imposed by force becomes burden disguised as gift. You cannot be charged for what you never asked for.

To rebut these assumptions, you must first understand them as commercial offers. Each notice from council is statement that says, "We believe you have received benefit by occupying property within our jurisdiction, and we demand payment in return." When you reply with questions rather than silence, you remove the foundation of belief. You shift matter from assumption to evidence.

Your first notice should always be peaceful. Acknowledge receipt of their letter and express willingness to settle any lawful obligation upon proof of claim. Then ask for specific evidence of contract. Request copy of agreement bearing your signature and the council's. Ask for breakdown of services provided, itemising value received. Require confirmation that you consented to those services. These requests are lawful and reasonable. Without answers, there is no proof of obligation.

Silence or evasion from the council confirms dishonour. They will often reply with references to legislation rather than contract. This response avoids question entirely. Legislation governs persons, not living beings. When no signed agreement exists, their claim collapses under its own weight. The council cannot provide proof of consent because none was ever given. The process survives only through assumption of ignorance.

Occupancy itself carries no lawful meaning. You may live in property, but that does not make you tenant of council. You are not using their land or resources directly. Property tax assumes ownership by council over all land, yet that ownership is never proven. In truth, the land belongs to the people collectively. Councils act as administrators, not proprietors. They cannot charge private individuals for living peacefully on earth.

The presumption of benefit also falls when examined logically. Councils claim to provide services for community, not individual. You cannot measure what portion of that service benefits you personally. They may collect waste from street, but you already pay for waste disposal through other taxes. They maintain roads, but roads are used by all. No contract exists linking your personal use to specific payment. Without measurable benefit, there is no lawful debt.

When writing your notice, include questions that expose this gap. Ask for evidence that services were requested by you personally. Request proof that you agreed to pay for them under threat of penalty. Ask for itemised statement showing direct benefit to you. End with statement of peace: "This communication is made in honour and with goodwill." These words preserve calm while demanding truth.

If council continues to send demands without answering, you may issue notice of fault. State that absence of proof confirms no lawful contract exists and that further claims will constitute harassment. Provide reasonable time to correct error. If silence persists, issue decree of closure declaring matter settled in peace. Keep all copies and proof of delivery. Your archive becomes evidence that you acted lawfully.

It is important to understand that rebutting assumption does not mean rejecting community. The Sovereign supports fairness and voluntary cooperation. You may still choose to contribute to local projects or charities, but by free will, not coercion. True community thrives on consent, not compulsion. When councils act through threat, they destroy spirit of service they claim to uphold.

You will often hear argument that living within area automatically makes you beneficiary of services. This logic fails under basic law. You may walk past public park, but that does not mean you requested its creation. You may see streetlight, but you did not contract for its maintenance. Benefit without request cannot create debt. If it could, every advertisement or unsolicited product would impose payment. Law forbids such practice in commerce. Councils violate that principle daily.

Rebutting assumption requires patience. Councils rarely admit error openly. They rely on repetition of policy to exhaust your resolve. Stay consistent. Respond once per communication, always within reason, always in peace. Over time, record of silence grows stronger than any reply. The more they avoid questions, the more their dishonour becomes visible.

You may also choose to include affidavit of non-benefit in your correspondence. This document states that you have not requested or accepted any specific service from council and that no contract exists between you. Once signed and witnessed, it stands as legal evidence unless rebutted by sworn testimony. Councils will not provide such testimony because no officer wishes to swear to untruth. Their silence again confirms your position.

The presumption of occupancy extends to tenants and homeowners alike. Councils send demands to whomever they believe resides at address. This assumption ignores reality of private ownership. The man or woman who purchased property already paid duties, fees, and taxes during transaction. Council tax adds second layer of payment without fresh consent. It is double charge disguised as civic duty.

To expose this, ask for proof of ownership by council over your private dwelling. Request evidence that they hold superior title to your land or home. Without such proof, their claim of authority fails. No man or woman may impose tax on property they do not own. Councils act as if they hold title through legislation, but legislation cannot override natural right of possession.

When you respond with these questions, always remain respectful. Officials reading your letters are human beings following instruction. Many do not understand difference between statute and law. Your calm tone teaches by example. Anger invites dismissal. Peace invites reflection. Each letter becomes small lesson in honour for those who receive it.

Rebutting assumption also requires inward honesty. If you genuinely use council services by choice, acknowledge it. You may agree to pay portion voluntarily as act of goodwill. Sovereignty is not escape from responsibility. It is freedom to decide based on truth. The difference lies in consent. You pay because you choose, not because you fear.

The next section will show how to combine this understanding with practical remedies such as affidavits and declarations of truth. You will learn how to turn absence of response into lawful evidence and how to protect your standing without aggression. Once you master this process, every assumption collapses under light of awareness, and peace replaces conflict.

The presumption of occupancy and benefit survives only because people rarely question it. The system counts on habit. Each year bills arrive, and each year payments are made. No one asks to see the original contract or to identify the living claimant. Yet every demand for council tax is built on the same unproven ideas, that your address equals agreement and that your silence equals consent. Once you recognise this, you hold the key to ending the illusion.

To rebut assumption, you must first return communication to realm of evidence. The council's letters are statements of belief, not proof. They state that you owe money because you occupy property. You reply not with denial but with lawful questions. Ask who claims ownership of the land. Ask who provided the benefit. Ask where the signed contract can be found. These questions turn belief into burden of proof.

When council cannot answer, it reveals itself as corporation seeking profit, not public body enforcing law. Their employees act as revenue agents, not peace officers. They follow script written to secure compliance, not truth. By keeping correspondence peaceful and factual, you remove the emotional energy that sustains illusion. Anger feeds authority. Calmness exposes it.

The idea of benefit is weakest part of their claim. Benefit must be tangible and measurable. If service cannot be valued individually, no lawful debt arises. Councils fund collective projects, not private contracts. They maintain parks, roads, and lighting for community as whole. You cannot be charged personally for fraction of collective service you never requested. This logic, though simple, dismantles foundation of tax.

Include these points within your correspondence. You might write, "I have not requested nor consented to any individual service from your corporation, and I require evidence of any contract or agreement showing personal benefit." Keep tone neutral. You are asking question, not accusing. Law rewards clarity.

Some officials may reply that statute grants them authority to charge. This answer avoids question because statute governs persons, not living beings. When you ask for contract and receive citation of policy, you expose misdirection. Repeat question once more. After second silence or avoidance, record that they failed to provide evidence. Your record now holds higher authority than their assumption.

You may also ask for proof of cost of services provided to your property. Demand itemised breakdown of lighting, waste collection, road maintenance, and other charges. They cannot supply it because services are funded from pooled accounts. Without individual contract or invoice, no lawful debt exists. Each unanswered question deepens silence that proves absence of agreement.

When preparing affidavit of non-benefit, state facts plainly. Declare that you have not requested or accepted specific services from council, that you have not entered contract for payment, and that no evidence has been presented proving obligation. Sign before witness. Serve copy on council and keep one in your archive. This affidavit stands as sworn testimony. Only sworn rebuttal from another living being can challenge it. Councils will not provide one because no officer wishes to swear to falsehood. Their silence therefore stands as admission.

Affidavits hold power because law recognises truth expressed under oath. Corporations cannot speak truth; only living beings can. When you create affidavit, you move matter from fiction to fact. You have now placed record of life above assumption of paper. That act alone changes energy of correspondence. The system senses awareness and retreats.

You will notice that the more questions you ask, the more generic council replies become. They use templates that avoid substance. This pattern shows weakness, not strength. Bureaucracy cannot think. It repeats. Each repetition strengthens your record because it proves absence of engagement. By maintaining patience and precision, you build unshakable evidence of dishonour.

Another common tactic is referral to enforcement agents. Councils pass matter to third party claiming to act on their behalf. Yet no contract exists between you and that agent. You may reply with simple question, "Please provide proof of lawful assignment and evidence that original obligation exists." Without such proof, their claim is void. Debt cannot be assigned when it never existed. The agent's authority ends with your question.

You may also encounter claim that by residing within borough, you accept its laws and duties. This statement confuses geography with contract. Presence in area does not create agreement with corporate entity managing that area. You are not their employee or tenant. You are living being occupying space on earth. Jurisdiction based on location is political fiction, not law. Consent remains cornerstone of all lawful obligation.

It is worth remembering that rebuttal of assumption must always be peaceful. You do not resist officers physically or threaten anyone. You respond with letters, affidavits, and notices. The power lies in paper backed by truth. Violence invites chaos. Calm correspondence restores order. The goal is correction, not rebellion.

If the matter ever reaches hearing, your record will speak louder than words. Present copies of all notices served, all unanswered questions, and affidavit of non-benefit. These documents show that you acted lawfully and sought evidence. The council's silence reveals absence of contract. Even within administrative systems, such record carries weight because it exposes lack of due process.

The presumption of benefit also fails under principle of fairness. A man or woman cannot be forced to pay for unwanted service. In commerce, unsolicited goods cannot be charged. In morality, gift given without request carries no expectation of return. Councils cannot transform imposition into contract. Their moral argument collapses when seen in light of law.

When corresponding, remind them gently that you respect genuine community service and are willing to contribute voluntarily where agreement exists. This statement removes accusation and shows good faith. Honourable tone disarms hostility. It demonstrates that your goal is fairness, not avoidance. Law always favours balance.

You may wish to end correspondence with declaration such as, "I stand in peace, wishing no conflict, but I require truth. Without proof of contract or measurable benefit, I cannot in honour confirm liability." This sentence captures essence of lawful living. It respects principle of peace while asserting boundary of consent.

Over time, this understanding changes how you view all obligations. You begin to recognise difference between contribution and compulsion. True community thrives on contribution. Compulsion destroys it. When enough individuals act from knowledge rather than fear, councils must eventually transform their methods. Awareness spreads slowly but inevitably.

Rebutting assumption is not act of defiance but act of education. You are teaching system that law still exists beyond policy. Each letter you send becomes lesson in conscience for those who read it. The world changes through small acts of truth repeated by many. You become part of that quiet restoration.

The next chapter will expand on these principles by exploring how to use affidavits and declarations of truth as lawful remedies. You will learn how to draft, serve, and preserve such documents so they stand as permanent record of honour. Once you understand this process, your words on paper will carry more power than any demand printed by a machine.

Chapter 10:
Common Law Remedies and Affidavits

Remedy is the heart of law. Without remedy, law is nothing more than empty promise. Every wrong must have means of correction, and every man or woman must have path to peace. The common law, older than government and simpler than statute, provides such path. It does not rely on complexity or authority. It rests on conscience, evidence, and honour. When councils or institutions act through assumption, remedy arises through written word of the living being.

The most powerful tool of remedy is the affidavit. It is the written truth of man or woman, signed, witnessed, and sworn under penalty of perjury. In common law, an unrebutted affidavit stands as truth in commerce. No court, council, or officer can overturn sworn statement unless they provide equal or higher evidence under oath. This principle places power back into hands of the living. It reminds the world that truth spoken in peace holds higher authority than policy written in fear.

An affidavit serves several purposes. It creates record of fact, it declares knowledge of truth, and it establishes your standing. When councils operate through presumption, affidavit removes doubt. It replaces assumption with evidence. Where bureaucracy speaks in policy, the living being speaks in truth. The difference is profound.

To create affidavit, begin with clarity. State your full living name as author. Declare that you are man or woman, not legal person. Affirm that you act in honour, seeking peace and fairness. Then state facts in numbered paragraphs, one point at a time. Each paragraph must be statement you know to be true. Avoid speculation or emotion. Fact is stronger than argument.

For example, you may write:

1. I am living man known as Roger of the family Davies.
2. I have received letters from corporation known as [Name of Council].

3. I have requested proof of contract and evidence of obligation.
4. No such proof has been provided.
5. I therefore declare that no lawful contract exists between me and said corporation.

Once facts are stated, include declaration of truth. Example: "I swear that the above statements are true and correct to best of my knowledge and belief." Sign the document before two witnesses or commissioner for oaths. Their signatures confirm that document was signed voluntarily and knowingly. Keep one copy for your archive and serve another on relevant party.

When served, affidavit becomes lawful evidence. If council disagrees, they must reply with counter-affidavit sworn under oath. They will not, because no officer wishes to swear personal responsibility for corporate claim. Their silence becomes acceptance of your truth. In law, silence after sworn testimony equals agreement. Thus affidavit transforms presumption into fact.

Affidavit also protects you in future correspondence. Once on record, it stands as statement of truth unless rebutted. Any further demand from council becomes act of dishonour because it ignores sworn evidence. You may reply with short notice reminding them that affidavit remains unrebutted and therefore stands as truth. This reminder often ends communication because no one can overcome it without oath.

Affidavits differ from notices. A notice communicates intention or question. An affidavit communicates truth. The notice asks for evidence. The affidavit declares evidence. Both together form complete remedy. Notice opens door to dialogue. Affidavit closes door to deceit.

In matters of council tax, affidavit of non-contract or affidavit of non-benefit are most relevant. They state that you have not entered contract with council and have not received individual service requiring payment. These affidavits, once served and unrebutted, render further claims null under common law. The council may continue procedure under statute, but their paperwork lacks lawful foundation.

Another form of remedy is declaration. A declaration is statement of belief or intent not necessarily sworn. It holds moral force though less than affidavit. You may use declaration to assert living status or withdraw consent from certain practices. Declarations work well when you wish to maintain peace without creating formal dispute.

Remedy also arises through notice of fault and opportunity to cure. This document reminds other party that they have failed to provide requested evidence and offers them chance to correct mistake. Honour requires that you always allow opportunity to cure before closing matter. This step prevents accusation of bad faith and strengthens your record.

After notice of fault, if silence continues, you may issue decree of closure. This final notice declares that all reasonable opportunities have been given and that matter is now settled in peace. Decree does not mean victory in conflict but completion of process. It brings closure both legally and emotionally. Peace returns because record is complete.

Common law remedy relies entirely on honour. You must act consistently and truthfully. False statements or exaggeration destroy standing. The power of affidavit comes from sincerity of its author. When you swear under oath, you invite judgment from conscience. If words are untrue, peace will not follow. Always speak only what you know. Truth requires no decoration.

Many people fear writing affidavits because they associate legal documents with complexity. In truth, simplicity carries more strength. One page of clear facts outweighs fifty pages of argument. Law recognises precision. Write in plain language. Avoid legal jargon. The goal is understanding, not intimidation.

Once you begin using affidavits, you realise how deeply law depends on record. Councils create their record through letters and computer systems. You create yours through notices and affidavits. The two records exist side by side. The question becomes which reflects truth. The one supported by oath always prevails.

It is also wise to understand moral aspect of remedy. The purpose of affidavit is not to attack but to clarify. You are not fighting councils but revealing truth. Each sworn statement reminds those in power that conscience still governs life. In time, even officials begin to recognise difference between authority and honesty.

Affidavits may also serve as protection for others. A parent may write affidavit of truth for family, declaring intent to live peacefully under law. A group of neighbours may sign joint declaration affirming right to fair treatment by local authority. Each document adds weight to collective awareness. Truth grows through repetition of honourable acts.

Common law remedy does not rely on courts to function. The living being who speaks truth already stands in court of conscience. When you write affidavit, you testify before that court. The paper is symbol of inner judgment. It carries weight because it reflects genuine understanding. This is why governments fear individual awareness. Systemic control fails when individuals act as law themselves.

Affidavit also serves spiritual purpose. It aligns word with truth. When you write, you bring thought into form. When you swear, you bind conscience to that form. This union of thought, word, and action creates power beyond bureaucracy. It is act of creation. Law responds to such creation because law is reflection of natural order.

The next section will show practical examples of affidavits and how they can be used in combination with notices to protect your standing. You will learn how to structure, serve, and preserve each document so that it becomes part of unbreakable record of honour. Once mastered, you will see that the living word carries more authority than any seal, statute, or policy ever written.

Every lawful process follows rhythm of offer, notice, proof, and closure. Affidavits and declarations form part of this natural rhythm. They are the bridge between conversation and evidence. Without them, correspondence remains opinion. With them, it becomes record. The living man or woman who masters this art moves from reaction to creation. They stop being subject of administration and become author of truth.

When using affidavits as remedy, structure and timing are essential. Each document you send must build upon the last. The first notice opens discussion. The second provides reminder. The affidavit concludes it. This steady approach demonstrates patience and fairness. It also prevents the council from claiming ignorance. They cannot say they were unaware of your position when record shows repeated communication.

When preparing affidavit, think of it as testimony before unseen jury of reason. The document must be clear enough that anyone reading it can understand without explanation. Avoid unnecessary quotations or complex references. Use short, direct sentences. Number each point to create order. Law respects order because order reflects truth.

An example of structure for affidavit of non-contract might read:

1. I am living man known as Roger of the family Davies.
2. I have received correspondence from corporation known as [Council Name].
3. Said correspondence claims financial obligation under title of council tax.
4. I have requested proof of contract establishing such obligation.
5. No proof has been provided.
6. I therefore declare that no lawful contract exists between myself and said corporation.
7. I affirm that this statement is made in peace and honour, without intent to deceive or cause harm.

The closing declaration should state: "I swear under full responsibility and liability that the above is true and correct to the best of my knowledge and belief." Sign in blue ink before two witnesses or commissioner for oaths. The blue ink symbolises living hand. Keep copies and note date of service.

Affidavit may also include attachment called exhibit, such as copies of letters or unanswered notices. Mark each as Exhibit A, Exhibit B, and so on. Reference them within text to show evidence of process. Exhibits strengthen your position because they show pattern of behaviour from council. Each unanswered letter becomes proof of silence, and silence equals agreement under law of commerce.

Once affidavit is complete, serve it on head of council or chief executive. Address it personally rather than to department. Delivery should be recorded. The moment it is received, time for rebuttal begins. Give them specific period, usually twenty-one days, to reply with counter-affidavit sworn under oath. If none arrives, your affidavit stands as truth. You may then issue final notice declaring it unrebutted and therefore accepted.

This process may seem formal, but its simplicity conceals great strength. Councils rely on assumption that individuals will never act in lawful form. When you present document written with calm authority, the tone of correspondence changes. You are no longer viewed as complainant but as equal. Systems that thrive on imbalance falter when faced with equality.

The moral power of affidavit lies in truth expressed without fear. Falsehood needs repetition to survive. Truth needs only to be stated once. When you declare it under oath, you seal it in conscience. This act carries more weight than any legal argument because it comes from life itself. Law follows life, not the other way around.

Common law remedy also includes right to contract privately. You may create private agreements between living beings that supersede corporate claims. For example, group of neighbours may agree to maintain their own waste collection or road maintenance. Such agreement removes need for council service and therefore for tax based on assumed benefit. Freedom grows through cooperation rooted in consent.

You can also use affidavit to correct public record. If false information has been entered in your name, such as claim of debt, you may serve affidavit of correction. State clearly that entry is false, that you have no contract creating liability, and that you require immediate removal of error. Once again, unless rebutted by sworn testimony, your statement stands. Record always yields to truth.

Another remedy under common law is notice of estoppel by acquiescence. This arises when one party remains silent after repeated opportunity to respond. After you serve notices and affidavit, if council continues to send demands without addressing substance, you may declare estoppel. This means they are legally and morally barred from repeating claim. Their silence became consent to your truth.

It is important not to confuse remedy with revenge. The purpose of these actions is peace. You seek closure, not victory. The man or woman who uses law to punish others becomes prisoner of same system they oppose. Honour requires mercy even towards those who act in ignorance. Each document you send should carry tone of goodwill. The system notices difference between hostility and clarity.

Over time, you will develop rhythm of lawful correspondence. Each demand will follow same pattern, and your replies will flow naturally. You will know when to write notice, when to serve affidavit, and when to close record. Fear of authority will disappear because you understand the process. That understanding is freedom in motion.

Keep all your documents organised. Create folder for each matter. Index letters by date and type. Include postal receipts and copies of envelopes. When everything is in order, you hold your own archive of law. Should any challenge arise, you can produce evidence instantly. The one who holds complete record always stands strongest.

Common law remedy teaches patience and restraint. Many seek quick results, but law moves at pace of truth, not desire. Silence from council may last weeks or months. Let it. The silence works for you. Every passing day without rebuttal strengthens your position. Peace is slow but sure.

Affidavit practice also encourages humility. Each time you write oath, you face your own conscience. You ask yourself whether words are true. That inner reflection purifies intention. It transforms legal process into spiritual discipline. The more truth you speak, the lighter you become. You realise that remedy begins within.

When used correctly, affidavits and declarations restore balance between individual and institution. They remind world that authority begins with life. Councils, corporations, and governments exist because living beings allow them. When those beings act again in honour, systems must adjust. That adjustment begins with written word of one person willing to stand in peace.

The next chapter will explore real examples of successful lawful defences and stories of men and women who used honour, patience, and written word to resolve matters peacefully. These examples will show that remedy is not theory but practice. When truth is lived, it becomes contagious.

Chapter 11:
Successful Lawful Defences and Examples

Proof of truth is found in experience. Law without demonstration is theory, and theory without evidence convinces no one. Across the country, ordinary men and women have used peace, honour, and written word to resolve disputes with councils and agencies without conflict. Their results differ, yet all share common thread. They acted with understanding. They wrote with precision. They remained calm when others reacted. In this chapter, you will read how lawful principles work when lived.

One man in the north of England began by questioning his annual council tax bill. Instead of paying automatically, he sent simple letter of conditional acceptance. He wrote that he was willing to settle any lawful obligation upon proof of contract. He asked for evidence of agreement bearing his signature and for identification of the living claimant. The council replied with printed copy of legislation. He sent second letter reminding them that statute is not proof of contract and asked again for evidence. No reply came.

After several weeks, the council issued summons. He responded with notice stating that without verified claim, he could not confirm obligation. He attended hearing by special appearance and asked whether court was court of record under oath. The clerk could not answer. The case was adjourned. Months later, the council quietly wrote off balance. No admission was made, no publicity sought, yet silence itself was victory. The process ended because proof never appeared.

In another case, woman in the Midlands used affidavit of non-benefit to challenge demand. She wrote sworn statement declaring that she had not requested or received individual service from council and had not entered any contract for payment. She served affidavit on chief executive and gave twenty-one days for rebuttal. None came. When reminder notice arrived, she replied once more, enclosing copy of affidavit and notice of fault. She received no further correspondence. Her record remains unrebutted to this day.

Such outcomes are not isolated. Similar patterns have emerged wherever people act calmly and document every step. Councils depend on assumption, not confrontation. They are trained to handle aggression, not awareness. When letters arrive written in language of honour, their scripts fail. There is no box on their forms for conscience.

One small business owner learned this during dispute over commercial rates. The council demanded payment under threat of enforcement. Instead of arguing, he wrote conditional acceptance and asked for proof that his company had signed contract for rates. The council produced no contract, only references to statute. He served notice of fault, then affidavit of non-contract. Months later, enforcement agents visited his premises. He handed them copy of affidavit and asked for signed warrant. They left without action. Silence followed. The account remains dormant years later.

Not every story ends quietly. Some councils continue sending letters even after lawful notices are served. In such cases, persistence matters. One couple in Wales exchanged more than ten pieces of correspondence before peace returned. Each time, they repeated same question: "Please provide proof of lawful obligation." Each reply from council avoided substance. After final notice of closure, they received no further demands. Their patience proved stronger than bureaucracy's persistence.

These examples share clear pattern. None of these men or women refused responsibility. They all expressed willingness to pay any lawful obligation. They did not hide, shout, or threaten. They asked questions. They created record. They held their ground in peace. That combination disarms system built on presumption.

Success in lawful defence depends less on clever words than on character. Calmness, consistency, and patience create authority. Councils are used to emotional letters filled with anger or denial. Such letters confirm stereotype of rebellion and justify continued pressure. When calm letter arrives written with clarity and respect, it disrupts expectation. Officials must either engage truthfully or expose themselves through avoidance.

Another lesson comes from community project in Scotland. Group of neighbours challenged local authority over new waste collection charge. They met weekly, studied law together, and drafted joint declaration. The declaration affirmed that they had never agreed to new charge and required council to produce proof of consent from each household. Signed by forty residents, the document was delivered in person to council office. After three months of silence, charge was suspended for review. The group later negotiated voluntary contribution plan instead of compulsory fee. Their unity turned demand into dialogue.

Lawful defence does not always mean total removal of payment. In some cases, resolution takes form of new agreement made in peace. One man in London offered small monthly payment based on voluntary contribution rather than statutory duty. He explained that he wished to support community but not under threat. The council, faced with his record of honourable communication, accepted arrangement quietly. He paid by choice, not fear. That distinction changed entire relationship.

Affidavits also play role beyond correspondence. In several instances, people have presented them directly in courtrooms. One man in northern city attended hearing with affidavit of truth stating that no contract existed. When clerk attempted to proceed, he placed copy on desk and said calmly, "Until this sworn statement is rebutted under oath, I see no jurisdiction." The clerk froze, unsure how to respond. The case was postponed and never resumed. The affidavit stood unrebutted.

It is important to remember that remedy comes from understanding, not imitation. You cannot simply copy another person's words and expect same result. Law responds to sincerity. Each notice and affidavit must reflect your own knowledge and intent. Truth cannot be memorised. It must be lived. Read, study, and understand before you act. The system recognises authenticity even when it cannot admit it openly.

There are also examples of partial success where process revealed truth but did not remove demand. In those cases, individuals still gained freedom from fear. They saw how authority depends on belief. One woman said that after serving notices, she continued paying to avoid confrontation but now does so with awareness. She no longer feels oppressed because she knows the nature of transaction. Knowledge itself became remedy.

The point of these stories is not to promise easy escape but to show pattern of empowerment. Lawful communication changes energy of relationship. It reminds councils that they are corporations accountable to people, not masters over them. It reminds individuals that peace is stronger than policy.

Those who act from anger often face resistance. Those who act from peace meet silence. Silence is not defeat; it is confirmation that truth requires no argument. Each unanswered notice proves that system has no answer to honour.

The final examples come from abroad, where similar principles have been used against property taxes and fines. In every instance, success depended on documentation, respect, and refusal to enter conflict. Whether in England, Australia, or Canada, the process remains same. Law follows conscience everywhere because conscience is universal.

These experiences prove that lawful remedy is not fantasy. It is living practice grounded in record, patience, and peace. The man or woman who follows it does not fight system; they outgrow it. Each letter they write, each question they ask, shifts balance of authority from assumption to truth.

The next section will explore how to stand in honour without fear. It will show how to maintain peace when challenged, how to act when silence breaks, and how to hold your position when others misunderstand your path. True sovereignty is not measured by victory in argument but by calmness under pressure.

The strongest lawful defences share common qualities: awareness, patience, record, and peace. They do not rely on drama or secrecy. They rely on truth expressed consistently. The men and women who achieve success do so quietly, without confrontation, and without boasting. They understand that victory through peace endures longer than victory through defiance.

The first quality, awareness, means knowing what you are doing and why. Many who fail attempt to use words they do not understand. They repeat phrases learned online without study. Councils recognise imitation and dismiss it. Awareness gives words meaning. Before sending any notice, read it aloud. If you cannot explain each sentence in plain language, do not send it. True law lives in comprehension, not repetition.

The second quality, patience, allows process to unfold. Councils move slowly, and silence can last for months. Those who rush lose balance. Honour requires giving other party fair time to respond. The living man or woman who acts with patience gains moral authority. Silence becomes ally, not frustration. The longer absence of reply continues, the stronger your position grows.

The third quality, record, transforms thought into evidence. Words spoken fade. Words written endure. Keep every letter, receipt, and envelope. Create timeline of events. This timeline is your shield. Should matter ever be questioned, you can produce proof of each step. Councils rely on people losing documents or forgetting dates. Order defeats chaos.

The final quality, peace, is foundation of all others. Peace removes fear. Fear clouds judgement and invites mistakes. When you act from peace, tone of your letters changes. Even hostile officials sense calmness and soften. The power of peace is invisible yet undeniable. It turns confrontation into conversation.

One man from Devon learned this through hardship. He began his journey angry at injustice and wrote aggressive letters. The council responded in kind. Threats escalated. Eventually, he stopped, reflected, and began again with humility. He rewrote notices in language of peace and respect. Within three months, correspondence ceased. Later, he received apology from junior officer for misunderstanding. The same system that resisted anger yielded to calmness.

Another example involves retired couple who faced enforcement over disputed balance. They did not panic. They invited agents to provide lawful warrant signed by judge of record. When none was shown, they served notice of trespass in peace. The agents left quietly and never returned. The couple continued correspondence with council until case was withdrawn. Their strength came not from confrontation but from calm certainty.

These stories show that lawful defence is internal discipline as much as external process. Each step tests patience, courage, and clarity. Councils operate on mechanical procedure. They cannot process conscience. When confronted by living beings who act with awareness, the machinery slows. It cannot harm what it cannot understand.

There is deeper lesson in these examples. Remedy is not always about stopping payment or erasing debt. Sometimes it means transforming relationship between you and authority. A man who understands law no longer fears government. A government that faces aware people must reform. Change begins not through protest but through understanding. Every letter of honour you send contributes to that transformation.

Groups that study and practise together often find faster progress. Shared knowledge creates support. When one member loses confidence, others remind them of truth. Councils are more cautious when faced with informed community than isolated individual. Unity amplifies peace. One voice may be ignored, but many calm voices create movement.

Lawful defence also benefits from public transparency. Those who act in truth need not hide. Keeping open record of communication, signed and dated, shows integrity. Deception hides in darkness. Truth thrives in light. When councils realise that you document everything, they proceed with care. Record is silent teacher.

It is also wise to avoid boasting about outcomes. Each success is private lesson, not trophy. Sharing stories to educate others is honourable. Sharing them to prove superiority feeds ego and weakens peace. The Sovereign acts quietly, guided by conscience, not applause.

A young woman from Yorkshire discovered this balance. After resolving dispute peacefully, she began helping neighbours understand notice process. She never told them what to do, only explained how she found peace through knowledge. Her small group grew into community study circle. They meet monthly to read maxims of law and discuss honourable living. Their focus is education, not rebellion. Change flows naturally from such purpose.

There are also lessons from failure. Some individuals fall into trap of argument. They write endless letters quoting complex laws or ancient documents. Councils respond with standard replies, and frustration grows. Lawful process ends where emotion begins. Simplicity always prevails. One letter written in plain truth outweighs many written in anger. The law of honour favours clarity over cleverness.

Another common error is mixing legal advice with lawful principles. The two belong to different worlds. Legal argument accepts jurisdiction of statute. Lawful communication stands outside it. When you argue law, you confirm their system. When you state truth, you remain free of it. Choose one path and stay consistent.

The essence of lawful defence is not to win but to restore balance. Each man or woman who acts with honour becomes living example of freedom in peace. Even when councils persist, your calmness affects those within system. Some officers later leave their jobs or question policy. The ripple of awareness spreads unseen yet unstoppable.

These experiences also show that remedy cannot be bought or delegated. Many search for quick solution through templates or representatives. True remedy requires personal action. Only you can write your truth. Others may guide, but no one can stand for you. Law recognises individuality because law itself arises from life. When you act in your own name with conscience, you embody living law.

The long-term effect of such practice is cultural change. Systems built on assumption begin to falter as awareness spreads. Councils become cautious. Language in letters softens. Some adopt voluntary schemes or mediation programmes. These small adjustments mark beginning of wider transformation. Lawful living reshapes governance by removing fuel of fear.

The final lesson from these examples is gratitude. Even confrontation with councils serves purpose. It forces you to learn patience, clarity, and truth. Each challenge becomes teacher. The more you practise peace under pressure, the stronger your understanding grows. Authority outside you mirrors authority within. When inner order is firm, outer control loses hold.

These real stories prove that common law remedy is not fantasy. It is living practice grounded in patience, communication, and conscience. Every man or woman who walks this path adds strength to collective awakening. The change is not loud or dramatic. It is quiet, steady, and inevitable.

The next chapter will guide you through final steps of this journey, showing how to live in honour without fear, how to balance freedom with responsibility, and how to stand as example of peace in a world that has forgotten it.

Chapter 12:
Standing in Honour Without Fear

Fear is the root of control. It is the quiet tool that keeps free men and women obedient. The system does not rule through force alone; it rules through suggestion, letters, and tone of threat. It counts on fear to fill gaps where truth should be. Once fear disappears, authority weakens. The final step of lawful living is therefore to stand in honour without fear. This is not act of rebellion but act of remembrance. You remember who you are.

Fear arises when man forgets his own authority. The living being was created before any government, law, or institution. All systems exist to serve life, not to rule it. Councils, courts, and corporations are inventions. They exist because living beings imagined them into being. When you recall this, fear loses its grip. The machine serves you; it cannot own you.

To stand without fear, you must trust process of law itself. True law protects the peaceful. The one who acts in honour, harms no one, and communicates truthfully has nothing to fear. Councils threaten enforcement because they assume guilt. Law, however, recognises only evidence. When you respond calmly, asking for proof, you stand in light of evidence. Fear retreats into shadow of ignorance.

Honour and fear cannot coexist. To act in honour means to tell truth even when uncertain. It means to keep record even when tired. It means to reply to letters rather than ignore them. Honour is consistency of conscience. When conscience governs, fear has no space. The man who knows he has acted rightly walks through challenge with peace.

Practical steps help remove fear. Keep your documents in order. Know what to write, when to send, and what it means. Preparation builds confidence. Confusion feeds fear; clarity starves it. Create folder for every matter. Number each letter, record each date, and note each silence. When the system attempts to intimidate you, you will see your record and remember truth. Facts restore calm faster than emotion.

Silence used with awareness also defeats fear. There is time to write and time to be still. Once you have served your notices and affidavits, let peace do the work. The system may send letters repeating same words. Do not react. Each repetition is sign of weakness, not strength. The council writes because it has no answer. Reply only when new information appears. The ability to wait is mark of mastery.

Standing without fear also means seeing officials as human beings. Behind every title is person doing job, often without understanding. When you treat them with respect, their hostility softens. Fear sees enemy; honour sees reflection. You teach them by example, not by lecture. Every calm conversation plants seed of awareness in heart of bureaucracy. Some seeds take years to grow, but all grow eventually.

The greatest obstacle to honour is anger disguised as righteousness. Many who learn about sovereignty begin by wanting to fight. They see injustice and wish to attack it. Yet anger binds you to what you oppose. The system feeds on conflict. It requires resistance to justify its existence. When you stop resisting, it loses purpose. Peace ends tyranny by making it unnecessary.

To live without fear does not mean ignoring danger. It means facing it with awareness. You may still receive letters or visits. You may still face misunderstanding. Yet when you know who you are, those events become tests, not threats. Each test invites deeper calm. Each moment of calm strengthens authority of conscience.

Honour is not weakness. It is strength under control. It allows firmness without aggression. When you act in honour, you keep promises, speak truth, and cause no harm. Councils and courts are powerless against such character. They rely on dishonour to function. The living being who keeps honour removes their fuel.

You may feel alone on this path. Most people around you still believe in authority of paper. They may question your choices or call you foolish. Do not argue. Live example quietly. In time, they will see peace on your face and wish to know its source. Truth persuades through calm presence, not through noise.

Honour also means accepting responsibility for consequences of your actions. Freedom without responsibility becomes chaos. If you make mistake, correct it quickly. If you cause harm, apologise and make amends. Law forgives those who act in truth. Fear hides error; honour admits it. The one who admits fault early never becomes slave to guilt.

To stand in honour without fear also requires daily discipline. Begin each morning with clarity. Write short statement of intent, such as "Today I act in peace and speak only truth." This simple act aligns mind with law. Throughout day, notice how often fear tries to intrude. Each time, pause and breathe. Fear cannot survive awareness.

Some people imagine that living without fear means never feeling it. In reality, it means recognising it and choosing peace instead. Courage is not absence of fear but mastery of it. When letter arrives bearing official seal, your body may react. That is natural. Read it slowly, breathe, and remember who you are. Paper has no power over truth.

Honour also requires faith in timing. Remedy does not always appear instantly. Sometimes peace takes months to manifest. Trust that process works even when unseen. Law follows rhythm of nature. Seeds planted today bloom tomorrow. Each letter written in peace becomes seed. Do not dig it up with worry. Let it grow in silence.

Living without fear changes how you perceive world. Threats lose meaning. Authority becomes service. You see councils not as enemies but as systems waiting to remember conscience. You begin to thank them for giving you opportunity to practise patience. Each challenge becomes teacher. Gratitude replaces resentment.

Honour protects not only you but those around you. Family and friends observe your calmness and feel safer. They may not understand your process, yet they sense peace it brings. Your example teaches without words. Children who see their parents act with honour grow into adults who respect truth. The world transforms one household at a time.

Standing without fear also means knowing when to walk away. Some battles are not worth energy. When matter no longer serves growth, close it with dignity. Write final letter of peace, store record, and move forward. Freedom lies in ability to release past. The council may continue its process, but your journey continues elsewhere.

The deeper meaning of honour lies in service. Freedom is not solitary. It is gift to be shared. The man or woman who finds peace has duty to help others find it. You do not impose beliefs but offer understanding when asked. Service grounded in humility strengthens peace.

The next section will complete this book with final reflections on freedom, honour, and the quiet power of written word. It will remind you that sovereignty is not goal but state of being, one lived daily through choice, awareness, and peace.

Standing in honour without fear is more than response to council letters. It is way of living. It becomes habit of mind that touches every part of life. The same calmness that answers a demand also shapes conversation with neighbour, family, or stranger. Once you live from honour, fear loses territory. Every breath becomes quiet declaration of sovereignty.

To live this way requires honesty with yourself. Fear often hides behind excuses. It whispers that peace will not work or that system is too strong. These voices belong to habit, not truth. Habit wants safety in submission. Truth invites freedom through responsibility. When you face fear and act in spite of it, the habit begins to dissolve.

The first step is trust in your own word. When you promise something, keep it. When you say you will reply, reply. When you commit to truth, hold to it even when others laugh. Keeping your word builds self-trust. The man or woman who trusts themselves does not fear authority. They know that law begins in conscience, not office.

The second step is self-education. Fear fades as knowledge grows. Read not only books of law but also writings on philosophy, peace, and human nature. The more you understand, the less mystery surrounds power. Councils and courts operate through predictable process. Once understood, it no longer intimidates. Education is light that reveals how small the shadow of fear truly is.

The third step is stillness. Before responding to any challenge, pause. Sit quietly and breathe. Stillness allows truth to rise. Reaction strengthens illusion. Reflection restores law. Many mistakes are made in hurry. The living man or woman who pauses before acting never falls to fear.

You will notice that fear feeds on imagination. It invents outcomes that have not happened. The letter arrives, and mind creates story of loss or punishment. Yet these stories exist only in thought. Law operates on evidence, not imagination. When you remember this, fear dissolves. Nothing exists until proven. The living being lives in now, not in fear of what may come.

Honour demands consistency even in private. Speak truth when no one hears. Keep peace in moments unseen. This integrity builds unseen shield. Councils cannot harm man whose conscience is clean. Every action aligned with truth strengthens protection. Law respects honesty because honesty mirrors natural order.

Standing without fear does not mean you never doubt. Doubt visits all who walk this path. The difference lies in response. The unaware man runs from doubt. The aware man listens to it and answers with truth. Doubt becomes teacher reminding you to stay awake. Each time you overcome it, confidence deepens.

When you meet others who share similar journey, support them. Many awaken alone and feel isolated. Simple conversation or shared understanding restores courage. Lawful living grows stronger through fellowship. Groups based on peace and respect can achieve far more than individuals acting in anger. Each supports the other, reminding that fear is illusion shared by many but mastered by few.

You will also encounter opposition. Some will mock ideas of sovereignty or lawful standing. They defend the system that enslaves them because it feels safe. Do not argue. Pity them kindly. Their ridicule means they have not yet faced their own fear. When they do, they may remember your calmness. Your example will become their first step to freedom.

One of the strongest protections against fear is gratitude. Each challenge reveals truth. Each confrontation teaches patience. When you thank the process instead of cursing it, energy changes. Fear cannot live in thankful heart. Gratitude transforms obstacle into opportunity. When you can thank council for teaching you peace, you have truly mastered law.

Honour also means knowing your limits. You are not required to fix the world. Your task is to live truthfully in your circle. Each act of honesty ripples outward. Freedom is not grand event but quiet accumulation of small acts done well. The man who writes one letter in peace changes world more than crowd shouting in anger.

Standing without fear also reshapes how you view wealth and success. You stop measuring freedom by possessions. You begin to value clarity, time, and peace more than money. True wealth is ability to sleep without worry, speak without deceit, and walk without guilt. The council can send as many letters as it wishes; none can take that from you.

The sovereign life is not retreat from world. It is participation without attachment. You engage with system when necessary but never forget it serves you. You use tools of law, not to dominate, but to remind others of balance. Honour and peace become daily practice, not slogans.

Some who walk this path fear making mistakes in paperwork or language. They worry that one wrong word will undo everything. This fear also belongs to system. It teaches perfectionism to create paralysis. In truth, intention matters more than form. A letter written sincerely in good faith carries more power than flawless document written in fear. Law responds to spirit, not style.

As you grow in understanding, you will see that fear once served purpose. It protected you before knowledge came. Now knowledge has replaced it. Fear becomes unnecessary. You thank it and let it go. What remains is calm certainty that truth governs all things.

To stand in honour without fear is to stand in love. Love for truth, for peace, for creation. This love is not sentimental; it is strength disguised as kindness. It forgives councils, clerks, and judges because it recognises ignorance as temporary. No one stays blind forever. When light arrives, even those who enforced injustice will awaken. Your peace hastens that moment.

The journey of lawful living ends where it began: within. Paper, notices, and affidavits are tools, not masters. The real work happens inside you. When conscience rules thought and word, the world outside aligns naturally. Councils cannot harm what is already whole.

Freedom is not escape from duty but understanding of it. You owe debt only to truth. Pay that debt daily through integrity, patience, and peace. Every letter you write, every step you take, every breath you draw in awareness pays that debt in full. The system fades into background of life, replaced by quiet confidence of self-rule.

Standing in honour without fear means never bowing to illusion again. You do not reject authority; you reveal its rightful place as servant of people. You do not hate those who act unjustly; you remind them through example that law begins and ends in heart.

The man or woman who masters this stands taller without raising voice. They command respect without demand. Their peace fills rooms where conflict once lived. Their words carry weight because they are born from silence. This is the living definition of sovereignty.

When you reach this point, council letters, taxes, and threats lose meaning. You will still act, still reply, still maintain record, but without tension. You have remembered truth behind form. Authority no longer controls you because it no longer lives inside you. Freedom is inward state reflected outward through calm action.

Standing in honour without fear does not end challenge; it transforms it. Each new event becomes opportunity to prove peace real. You stop asking world to change and start being the change. Law becomes natural expression of who you are. You embody the living law.

The next and final section of this book will gather all lessons together into reflection on freedom, law, and community. It will remind you that sovereignty is journey without end, walked daily with awareness and peace.

Final Thoughts

Freedom is not destination. It is discipline lived one moment at a time. Many begin this path believing they will one day receive document declaring them sovereign or letter confirming independence from system. They imagine single event that ends all struggle. Yet freedom does not arrive from outside. It unfolds quietly from within. Each choice to act in truth, each letter written in peace, each moment spent without fear, builds foundation of sovereignty.

The purpose of this book has been to remind you that the power to live lawfully and peacefully already belongs to you. Councils, courts, and governments operate through assumption. They expect obedience because obedience has become habit. The living man or woman who remembers truth breaks that habit simply by asking question. Law is not cage; it is mirror. When you stand in truth, it reflects peace back to you.

You have learned that contracts, not threats, create obligation. You have seen how councils act as corporations making offers, not as masters issuing commands. You have understood that silence is not weakness but powerful tool of honour. When used with awareness, silence exposes deceit.

You have also learned practical structure of remedy. Notice, conditional acceptance, affidavit, and declaration are steps of lawful communication. Together they form process of truth. When you follow these steps with calmness, every challenge becomes test of peace rather than battle for control. This process transforms fear into understanding.

Remember that councils and officials are people caught in system of habit. Most act without malice. They do not know difference between statute and law. Your letters may be first time they see distinction between person and living being. You are not their enemy; you are their reminder. When you act in peace, you hold mirror before them. Some will ignore it; others will awaken. Both reactions serve purpose.

The Sovereign life is not about isolation from society. It is about participation in awareness. You still communicate, trade, and cooperate, but with clear boundaries. You know where authority ends and where conscience begins. You no longer confuse policy with law or silence with consent. You live with open eyes.

You will still face misunderstanding. Some will call you dreamer or troublemaker. Others will insist that statute is supreme. Their words cannot touch truth. Freedom does not require recognition from those who fear it. You need no validation from paper or office. The living being carries authority by birth.

Sovereignty demands humility. To live free means to accept full responsibility for choices. There is no one to blame, no one to hide behind. You cannot curse government for errors you continue to support through fear. Freedom begins when you stop expecting rescue and start acting in honour. The greatest revolution happens quietly inside.

Community built on such individuals cannot be controlled. Councils lose power when people act in peace together. When neighbours support one another, systems of coercion weaken. They cannot divide community grounded in trust. The future belongs to those who build cooperation from consent rather than authority from fear.

You may wonder whether peace alone is enough to change world. History answers yes. Every movement that lasted began with idea expressed peacefully and lived consistently. Violence burns fast and dies quickly. Peace endures because it grows from understanding. Each notice you write, each affidavit you serve, each conversation held in patience adds to quiet revolution of conscience.

The principles shared in this book apply beyond council tax. They extend to banking, contracts, and daily life. Every interaction is opportunity to practise law of honour. When you say yes, mean yes. When you say no, mean no. When unsure, seek clarity before acting. These small habits build unshakable foundation. Law follows integrity as shadow follows light.

Keep record of all you do. Archive letters, notices, and replies. Your written word becomes map of journey. One day you will look back and see how far peace has brought you. Record also protects future generations. Those who come after will learn from your process and walk with more certainty.

Honour does not demand perfection. You will make mistakes, speak in haste, or forget detail. Forgive yourself quickly and correct path. Law allows correction because life allows growth. The man who learns from error grows wiser than one who never risks truth. Every challenge is opportunity to refine peace.

Do not fall into pride. Knowledge of law can tempt ego. It may whisper that you are superior to others. Remember that law exists to serve love, not pride. The truly sovereign man is humble. He helps others understand without boasting. His peace invites trust because it carries no judgment.

Living this way may bring loneliness at first. You will see through illusions that still comfort many. Yet solitude will pass. The world needs examples of honour more than ever. When you stand quietly in truth, others will find you. Like attracts like. True community forms naturally around shared peace.

If fear returns, as it sometimes will, remind yourself of truth. Paper cannot own life. Policy cannot bind conscience. Office cannot replace heart. Read your own notices aloud. Hear calmness in your words. They are echo of your higher self-reminding you that law lives within.

Freedom is not measured by what you refuse to pay but by how you live. The free man does not seek conflict. He seeks balance. He does not run from duty but chooses it consciously. He does not hate authority but restores it to rightful place beneath law. This is maturity of sovereignty.

The true victory is peace of mind. When you wake without dread of letter or knock, you have won. When you answer any challenge with calm and clarity, you have triumphed. The world outside may look unchanged, yet world within has transformed completely. No authority can undo that shift.

Carry forward what you have learned. Teach through example, not argument. Encourage others to ask questions, to read, to think. Do not force belief; offer knowledge. Every act of education weakens illusion of control. Systems fade when people remember truth.

This path never ends. Sovereignty is not goal but lifelong practice. You will meet new challenges, new forms of authority, new tests of patience. Each one gives chance to refine peace further. The living law grows with you.

When you next receive letter from council or agency, pause and smile. See it not as threat but as invitation to practise honour once more. Each demand becomes opportunity to confirm who you are. The cycle that once caused fear now strengthens peace. This is true mastery of law.

If this book has helped you reclaim calmness in face of authority, let that calmness spread. Share it with family, neighbours, and community. Let your peace become quiet example of strength. The world changes not through protest but through presence. Be that presence.

The journey ends where it began, with simple truth: you are living being, not corporate entity. You owe no debt except to conscience, no duty except to truth, no loyalty except to peace. Stand quietly, live honourably, and act with awareness. The law will recognise you because it was written in your nature before it was written on paper.

Walk forward in freedom, not shouting but knowing. Speak truth softly and live it fully. The system will fade into silence, and only peace will remain.

Don't miss out!

Visit the website below and you can sign up to receive emails whenever Roger Davies publishes a new book. There's no charge and no obligation.

https://books2read.com/r/B-A-HHGNE-VMDGH

Did you love *Council Tax Nullity: How to Challenge Local Tax Demands through Honour and Law*? Then you should read *Cease the Decree: Ending Contracts in Peace*[1] by Roger Davies!

[2]

What if the highest law was already written within you?

Cease the Decree is a profound exploration of peace, honour, and conscience. It guides the reader through a complete transformation of understanding, from fear of authority to the calm confidence of self-governance. The message is not rebellion but remembrance. You are already lawful because you are alive.

Across twelve chapters and a closing reflection, Roger Davies leads you through a process of awakening. You learn how to communicate with clarity, respond without hostility, and live in harmony with the Law of the Living. Each principle builds upon the last, showing that true freedom does not come from defiance but from awareness.

---

1. https://books2read.com/u/bOvqyA

2. https://books2read.com/u/bOvqyA

This is not a book about loopholes or technicalities. It is a study of conscience as the foundation of peace. The author explains how to stand with honour in every situation, how to speak truth in written form, and how to use silence as evidence of strength. Through stories, examples, and reflections, you see how ordinary moments become lawful acts when guided by integrity.

You will explore:• How to turn conflict into communication through written peace• The role of silence as agreement or boundary• The difference between truth and belief in lawful conduct• The meaning of forgiveness as the highest expression of authority• The power of private record and personal responsibility• How the Law of the Living governs all human interaction

Cease the Decree reminds the reader that law is not a system of control but a reflection of conscience. Governments and institutions depend on compliance, but conscience depends on awareness. When you act in peace, you reveal a different kind of power — one that cannot be taken or transferred.

This book belongs to the *Sovereign Action Series*, a collection that teaches living freedom through personal integrity and self-respect. Each volume focuses on a different aspect of lawful living, offering practical guidance grounded in philosophy rather than protest.

Roger Davies writes with calm precision, offering not argument but understanding. His words speak directly to those who feel disillusioned by authority yet seek a peaceful way to stand in truth. The path described here is demanding but attainable. It asks for discipline, patience, and compassion — the real tools of liberty.

Cease the Decree is more than reading material. It is an invitation to live differently. It reminds you that law without life is empty, but life guided by honour becomes the highest law of all.

Also by Roger Davies

Adventures in Sovereignty: Growing Up Free

The Secret of the Hidden Name

Sovereign Action

Cease the Decree: Ending Contracts in Peace

Council Tax Nullity: How to Challenge Local Tax Demands through Honour and Law

The Private Record: How to Build Lawful Evidence of Truth and Standing

Sovereign Foundations: Liberty, Rights, Consent

The Constitution of One: How the Bill of Rights Protects the Sovereign Man & Woman

From Subjects to Sovereigns: Reclaiming the Spirit of 1776

Liberty by Consent: Reclaiming Freedom Through the Law of Consent

Standalone

The Commonwealth Corporation: How Australia Was Turned Into a Business

The Legal Fiction: The Greatest Trick Ever Played on Humanity

The Sovereign Path: Living Free Beyond the System

Common Law: The True Law of the Living

Freedom by Rebuttal: How to Say No and Stand Free

The Magna Carta: Why It Is Important to Sovereign Men and Women
The Trust Game: Hidden Estates and the Cestui Que Vie Act
Freedom by Notice: Winning with Paperwork
The Hidden Contracts: How Governments Enslave the People
The Law of the Living: Admiralty Shadows and the Path to Sovereignty
Standing as a Living Man or Woman in Canada: Reclaiming Freedom Beyond Statutes and Policy
Sovereign Stories for Children: 14 Parables of Freedom, Truth, and Honour
The Definitive Sovereign Handbook: Do No Harm, Cause No Loss, Commit No Fraud

About the Author

Roger Davies researches the crossroads of commerce, policy, and personal sovereignty. He writes for readers who sense there is more to the story, who are ready to replace fear with honour and paperwork with plain truth. When not writing, he helps men and women organise their records, challenge unfounded claims, and build communities grounded in mutual aid and responsibility.

www.ingramcontent.com/pod-product-compliance
Lightning Source LLC
LaVergne TN
LVHW090417210926
848480LV00002B/597